The House Spirit

Kanoko Okamoto

Kanoko Okamoto with son Taro in 1919.

THE HOUSE SPIRIT
and other stories

Kanoko Okamoto

translated and with a biographical sketch by
Kazuko Sugisaki

A version of the biographical essay first appeared in *ANAÏS : An Interna-tional Journal*, Volume 12, 1994. "The River" first appeared in *ANAÏS : An International Journal*, Volume 1, 1983, and "The House Spirit" in *ANAÏS : An International Journal*, Volume 11, 1993.

Okamoto, Kanoko, 1889-1939
[Selections. English 1995]
The house spirit, and other stories / Kanoko Okamoto; translated and
with a biographical sketch by Kazuko Suksaki.
p.   cm.
Contents: Sushi — The old geisha (Rogi sho) — North country
(Michinoku) — The house spirit (Karei) — The river (Kawa).
ISBN 0-88496-392-6 (pbk.)
1. Okamoto, Kanoko, 1889-1939—Translations into English. 2. Okamoto,
Kanoko, 1889-1939—Biography. 3. Authors, Japanese 20th century—
Biography. I. Sugisaki, Kazuko. II. Title.
PL835.K3A27   1995

895.6'344—dc20   94-48092 CIP

CAPRA PRESS
P.O. Box 2068
Santa Barbara, CA 93120

CONTENTS

◆

A WRITER'S LIFE: KANOKO OKAMOTO

"Some day," she said, "we'll go to Paris."

Kanoko Okamoto was born on March 1, 1889, in the villa of her parents, Torakichi and Ai Ohnuki, at Aoyama, Tokyo. She was their third child and first daughter. At the age of two, in ill health, she was sent to live with a relative in Futako, hometown of the Ohnuki family. Today the area is a well-developed suburban district of Tokyo, but at the turn of the century it was still a small rural community near the Tama River, where the Ohnukis had lived for several hundred years as the largest landowners of the region. Kanoko's parents had thought it best to raise the sickly child in an environment close to nature.

Soon after Kanoko moved to Futako Village a governess was hired to look after her. She was the daughter of a scribe in the household of Satsuma, a feudal lord in Kyushu, and had been a lady-in-waiting to a princess of the lord before the Meiji Restoration abolished feudal clans. She was well read in Japanese and Chinese classical literature and an accomplished artist in the Noh dance (*shimai*), in brush calligraphy, and in the performance of the tea ceremony. A lady of impeccable manners herself, her educational methods were strict and thorough. Kanoko's mother, who bore a total of ten children over the years, was more than happy to entrust her oldest daughter to the care of her governess.

Before Kanoko learned to read, her governess recited passages from *The Tale of Genji* to her and made her repeat them. Instead of reading fairy tales to Kanoko at bedtime, the governess told her stories about modern Western civilization. At an early age, Kanoko was enrolled in a village school run by a Buddhist priest at a local temple. There she became acquainted with the classics of Japanese and Chinese literature and learned to recite ancient Japanese poems in the *waka* or *tanka* form of thirty-one syllables, collected in such volumes as *The Collection of Ten Thousand Leaves* (Manyoshu, ca. 795 A.D.) and *Ancient and Modern Poems* (Kokinshy, ca. 905 A.D.).

She practiced brush calligraphy, which her tutor taught her with particular zeal. When her bold, dashing strokes escaped over the edges of the paper, the tutor encouraged her boldness of spirit rather than trying to confine her into tight orderliness.

While her tutor imposed upon Kanoko a disciplined education, she also idolized the child and often called her "my princess" in front of other people. She taught Kanoko the Noh dance, dressing her in luxurious kimonos, which her father bought from the finest shops in Tokyo. She gave Kanoko bread and butter, milk and fruits for breakfast, instead of the traditional Japanese fare of rice and miso soup, believing they were hard to digest.

In 1896, when she was seven, Kanoko entered Takatsu Elementary School in Futako Village, but apparently after the teaching of her governess, there was little she could learn from this first exposure to conventional school.

In those early years, Kanoko often displayed her independent spirit. One day when she and her tutor encountered a band of dog catchers making the rounds of the neighborhood, Kanoko saw a poodle she sometimes took care of about to be rounded up. She ran toward the dog and flung herself over its body. The whip of a dog catcher grazed her back. The tutor was horrified and told her to let go of the dog. But Kanoko wouldn't move. With her hands and knees on the ground she protected the dog with her body until the dog catchers gave up and went away.

The young girl developed a perplexing eye disease. Her vision seemed to fade when her general physical condition weakened. The apprehensive parents withdrew her from the village school and sent her with her tutor to Tokyo, where she was to be treated by a noted eye specialist.

His office was near the center of the old downtown section of Tokyo and became Kanoko's first introduction to this area of the city. Kanoko was fascinated by the frequent festivals of small shrines and temples with their bustling display of street stalls, the voices of the goldfish peddlers and cotton candy merchants. When her eyes improved, Kanoko returned to Futako.

Soon she came under the influence of her elder brother, Shosen Ohnuki, a student of literature. Shosen was a brilliant young man, a member of a literary group that included Junichiro Tanizaki, later author of *The Makioka Sisters*. After finishing his elementary education in Futako, Shosen went to the Tokyo Senior High School, then entered the University of Tokyo, pursuing the best course of education. He introduced Kanoko to many French, Russian and American writers like Maupassant, Flaubert, Tolstoy, Turgenev and Emerson. He also introduced her to the Bible and took her to see Reverend Masahisa Uemura, a well-known Protestant minister at the time.

When Kanoko was seventeen, she and her brother joined the New Poetry Society, Shin-Shi-Sha, founded by a famous poet couple, Tekkan and Akiko Yosano, who also originated and edited the poetry magazine, *Myojo (The Morning Star)*.

A *tanka* poem by Kanoko in the July 1906 issue became her first appearance in print. Brother and sister pledged to each other to devote their lives to literature, to the special muse of poetry.

Kanoko entered Atomi High School for Women in Tokyo in 1902. Established in 1875 by a renowned painter, calligrapher and Confucian scholar, it was one of the oldest schools for women in Japan. Its goal was to give Japanese women a new education in line with the changing currents of the time while not neglecting traditional female virtues. Some three hundred young women from aristocratic and wealthy families attended the school and were known for their luxuriant and elegant attire.

At school, Kanoko sat quietly in the classroom and hardly participated in any of the activities. The school mistress suggested that the teachers leave her alone since the girl seemed to have some special qualities which she might develop better by herself. While at Atomi, Kanoko also began to study English at Sakurai English School where she met other women writers and artists who provided a welcome intellectual stimulus. Kanoko's *tankas* began to appear in magazines and newspapers.

Kanoko graduated from Atomi High School in March 1907 and soon met a dashing young art student, Ippei Okamoto, who attended Ueno Art College (then regarded as the best in Japan). They fell in love and, though her mother was ap-prehensive about Kanoko's lack of experience in running a household, they were married in 1910. As was the custom of the day, the newlyweds lived with the Okamoto family, with Ippei's parents and his two sisters. While their honey-moon days seen to have been quite happy, the conventional living arrangement was more than Kanoko could handle, and things did not improve when their first son, Taro, was born in February of the following year.

Ippei had just graduated from the College. The Tokyo Imperial Theater was under construction, and he was com-missioned to paint murals for the building. But this work was only temporary and he had not yet secured a regular job. Ippei's father, a calligrapher, saw his daughter-in-law suffering in silence, so he built a small house for the young couple using most of his savings.

Ippei's struggle as a young artist went on a few more years until a happy coincidence gave him the opportunity to illustrate a novel by the English scholar and author Soseki Natsume (1867-1916), which was serialized in the newspa-per, *Asahi Shimbun*. This brought him a permanent position at the newspaper where, branching out as a political car-toonist, he became an enormous success.

While his family income rapidly increased, Ippei always spent more than he earned not on his family but on his own

pleasures. A self-appointed playboy, he was keenly concerned not to lose face among his friends, whom he royally
entertained in high-class restaurants and geisha houses
while his family starved. In 1913, Kanoko had a second child,
but the little girl lived only eight months.

Left in the small house with her infant son and no money
for even the barest necessities, Kanoko, so childlike herself,
felt utterly helpless. Sitting in the dark, because the electricity had been shut off, Kanoko caressed her son and repeated
a monotonous chant: "Someday we'll go to Paris, someday
we'll go to Paris." Paris was the city of her dreams where all
the literary excitement was taking place.

Kanoko's *tankas* of that period were given the title *Nageki*
(Lamentation).

Kanoko, your bright eyes like the fruit of the loquat
Became exhausted in lamenting.

Kanoko, your birdlike songs died away,
and this fall became lonely ever more.

Kanoko, Kanoko, stop crying and sing a lullaby
to an infant child who lies by your side.[1]

Ippei's behavior, of course, deeply hurt Kanoko, but she was above all disappointed with him because she now realized that the artist she had seen in him did not really exist. In a letter to her brother Shosen she wrote that though Ippei still interested her as a person, his art would never go beyond the mediocre, and she implored her brother to guide her in the world of literature:

> I don't understand why I can be so base as to seek fame. But actually it is not the love of fame; it is that I cannot help doing something and I cannot help expecting the result of doing something to be recognized in the world. And that something for me must be literature.[2]

Her beloved brother died suddenly at the age of twenty-four, in 1912, when Kanoko was only twenty-two. Shosen's death was a devastating loss for her. He had been her confidante and her guide in literature, her artistic *raison d'être*. Now she was determined to carry on the pursuit of literature for both of them. Shosen's brief life had profoundly influenced Kanoko. One of the Japanese writers Shosen admired most was the poet and novelist Tohson Shimazaki (1872-1943), whose many works included the *romans fleuves*, *The Family* and *The Broken Commandment*. Kanoko's work shares a common theme with Shimazaki: the importance of the relationship between past and present reflected in individuals who are bound to their "family," the basic and concrete social unit in Japan.

When her mother died three months later, Kanoko was driven to the verge of insanity. Her son Taro recalled this nightmarish period in his essay "My Mother's Memory":

> Mother was almost insane. My playmates used to tease me, saying that mother was a ghost. As young as I was, I remember how humiliated I felt, but then, with her disheveled hair hanging down over her shoulders and the pale face with eyes that did not focus, she must have presented a weird appearance.[3]

In December 1913, Kanoko was hospitalized with a severe nervous breakdown. It took her several months to regain her health. When she returned home, spring had already arrived.

Watching his wife drive herself to the brink of insanity, Ippei realized for the first time the extent of Kanoko's emotional sensitivity and its possible destructive consequences. She could not take any emotion lightly—joy or sorrow, love or hate. Her passionate feelings penetrated the very core of her existence, and when they were directed toward a particular object she was blind to everything else. Ippei began to understand these qualities were rare and precious, to be protected at any cost. He vowed to help her and protect her as best he could so that her valuable personality would never be harmed again. Now their life together finally seemed to have achieved a new and peaceful intimacy with shared understanding and mutual respect.

Then, in 1915, another person entered their relationship. On an early summer day, Kanoko, looking out from an upstairs window, noticed a young man standing by the fence and hesitatingly looking at her window. Their eyes met and the young man blushed and ran away. A few days later he reappeared, still lingering at the fence. Kanoko invited him into the house.

The young man, Shigeo Horikiri, was himself a writer. He knew of Kanoko's poetry and told her he had a great admiration for her work. Kanoko was immediately attracted to the handsome young man. She recognized in him a delicate sensitivity, simple directness and devoted admiration for her. They often met in secret, it was a forbidden love.

Kanoko wrote many *tankas* during this period:

Mosquitos begin to buzz in a twilight-filled room,
We two remain silent, sobbing.

Upon my hand that holds an umbrella for you

Your soft tears are falling.

You have grown gaunt little by little
Entwined with my tender yet piercing eyes.

Kanoko could bear this secret love no longer and confessed it to her husband. Ippei's reaction was extremely
unusual. He suggested she introduce this young man to
him and, if she wished, bring him to live in their home,
since there was a spare room upstairs. With Ippei's permis-
sion, Shigeo came to live with the Okamotos. Ippei had given
up his drinking parties and was spending more time working in his studio. Upstairs, Shigeo was writing a novel, and
Kanoko served as a critic of his work, often quite a scathing
one.

This strange *ménage à trois* lasted for awhile, but one day
Ippei asked Kanoko to bring him the clothes he had worn
at their wedding, which were stored in a chest of drawers.
He put them on and left.

Ippei joined a troupe of *Kappore* dancers and soon became
one of the chief performers of this comical dance which sati-
rizes, with its deliberately sordid gestures, the loves and
lovers of the red-lantern district.

Left alone with Shigeo, Kanoko grew more possessive and
jealous of the young man. She wrote:

My jealousy so violent and tenacious
Till at last you are taken ill.

Ah, forgive me, I shall cry no more,
No longer jealous, I am a woman, nursing you gently.

Shigeo went home to Fukushima, a city in the north, where
he died of tuberculosis in the summer of 1917, at the age of
twenty-four. He left behind a short novel, *Winter*, which ex-
amines their turbulent relationship in scrupulous detail.
Kanoko wrote about Shigeo's death:

You alone are peacefully reposed parting from our world,
This autumn everything is crying.

"Alone in this world, how can I survive?" you wondered.
How much more difficult it must be alone in the
otherworld.

It was the love so close to your death,
Do not wonder then if it was a lonely one.

After Shigeo was gone, Kanoko and Ippei found themselves in the wreckage of love. Ippei realized that permit-
ting Shigeo to live with them had not made his wife happy.

She had her young man, but she also saw her husband suffer. Their second son, Kenjiro, born early in 1915, died six months later.

To save what was left of their marriage, they needed help. First they turned to Christianity. Kanoko took Ippei to see Reverend Uemura whom she had once visited with Shosen. After listening silently to their story, Uemura offered neither consolation nor judgment. He simply opened his Bible and started reading aloud.

From then on Uemura came to their house once a week to read the Bible with them. To Kanoko's insistent question of why an omnipotent God would create a human being so incomplete that he would sin, Uemura's response was always the same: study the Bible. As her study progressed she became more disquieted by such concepts as "sin," "damnation," "evil," and "doom." She felt that she was a woman who had sinned and would never be forgiven, never redeemed.

Ippei then led Kanoko to Buddhism. The couple went to meet Harada, the High Priest of Kenchoji Temple in Kamakura, capital of Japan in the Middle Ages. Soon Kanoko participated in a five-day sitting Zen. The Buddhist priest told her that anguish was invaluable, that her way of thinking was not mistaken, and that her honest and single-minded character was something precious. This was exactly what

Kanoko needed to hear. She drank these words like life-giv-
ing nectar and began her long pursuit of Buddhism.

Kanoko began with a study of Shinran (1173-1262), foun-
der of the Shin Sect, who led a reform movement during the
devastating civil war period. The movement, begun by his
own teacher, a priest named Honen (1133-1212), proclaimed
that the absolute salvation of all men depends not on their
"goodness" but on "another power," the Faith in Buddha.
Reading Shinran's *Tan I Sho* (*A Lament of Discrepancies about
Shinran's Teachings*), Kanoko came across the sentence: "Even
the good are saved, then why not the wicked?" In an essay,
"The Teaching of Shinran as Spiritual Manna," she recalled
the excitement she felt in reading this passage. She felt for
the first time that her scepticism was answered and that she
would really be saved, Buddhism never denies human nature but accepts it as inevitable.

She found another passage in *Tan I Sho* which appealed
to her:

Amida-Nyorai made it possible that when the wish to say
the prayer occurs to us, believing that we shall be saved in
the other world through the wondrous power of *Amida-
Nyorai*'s vow, we are immediately enveloped by the Great
Mercy that saves all without exception. We must be aware
that the *Amida-Nyorai*'s vow does not segregate the old from

the young, the good from the wicked. It requires only our faith because it is a vow that aims at saving sinners who accumulate sinful deeds and whose worldly desires are as strong as the flames of burning fire. If we believe in this vow there will be no need for us to accumulate good deeds in this world for there is absolutely no "goodness" superior to prayer. We must not be afraid of wickedness because there is no "wickedness" that hinders us from salvation by this vow of *Amida-Nyorai*.[4]

Kanoko's searching spirit eagerly absorbed these teachings. For the next ten years she read and studied a complete collection of Buddhist Sutras, Laws, and Treaties embodied in a famous work, under the supervision of a great Buddhist scholar, Junjiro Takakatsu, and began to write essays and give lectures on Buddhism. She wrote plays with Buddhist teachings as their theme and one was produced on stage with Kabuki actors.

As her studies and activities in Buddhism progressed, Kanoko was faced with a new problem: should she follow the path of a religious believer or that of an artist? After a long period of hesitation and indecision she came to the conclusion that she could not abandon either path. She would have to continue to speak out of Buddhist philosophy, through which her soul knew peace, but never could she abandon literature. She would speak on Buddhism through literature.

By 1926 her reputation as a Buddhist scholar as well as a *tanka* poet was well established. She was busy with lectures, broadcasting and writing. In an article for the *Yomiuri* newspaper, Kanoko summed up her position:

> I have been long aware of the existence of three independent elements within myself: the human, the religious and that of art. They have fought among themselves and tortured me. . . . But when I accepted their conflict as conflict, I began to value their separate identities. They no longer torture me. . . . Now I can meditate on religion from the human point of view, on art from the religious and on religion from the artistic point of view. I hope to approach the mysterious existence of all three elements. They are three, but they are also one and the same, and yet they should be expressed separately.[5]

When Kanoko's essays on religion were collected and published in a volume entitled *Sange Sho,* Ippei contributed an illustration to the book called *Kanoko Kannon* (Kanoko modeled after the Goddess of Mercy, Avalokitesvara). He explained that in the old days faithful believers created statues of the Buddhist saints in their own image so that their ties to the saints might be strengthened. Ippei wanted to do the same for Kanoko, and he felt she very much resembled the Goddess of the Jyoruriji Temple.

Ippei began to identify Kanoko with this Goddess of Mercy. He spoke of her as a saintly woman and after her death revealed that from then on the couple had no sexual relationship. Kanoko's physical appearance began to change. She gained weight, and her figure became plump and well-rounded. Her character also changed. She lost her nervous temperament and gradually acquired a rich, affable personality which Ippei called her *"Urmutter"* quality. He also began to emphasize Kanoko's childlike innocence and to address her even in public as "my dear daughter," while she, as some friends observed, called him "papa," in a most trusting manner. For Ippei, Kanoko now embodied three elements: *Urmutter*, the Goddess of Mercy, and the Innocent Child; but these three different qualities were unified in her by the insistent, order-giving, creative power of the artist.

In December 1929, the Okamotos started out on their first trip abroad. By then, Ippei was at the height of his career. His cartoons as well as his essays and stories had gathered an enthusiastic readership. The *Asahi Shimbun* chose Ippei to cover the Disarmament Conference held in London in 1930. Although they do not appear in the official records, or in Kanoko's account of the journey, two young men accompanied the Okamotos on their trip.

One of them was Yasuo Tsunematsu, the son of a rich landowner in Tottori and an old friend of Kanoko's father. Yasuo and his older brother, then students at Keio University, had come to live with the Okamotos in 1922. The older brother had died during an epidemic shortly after he arrived in Tokyo, but Yasuo, a gentle soul, had stayed on, helping Kanoko with household chores and gradually assuming the responsibility of managing family affairs. An accountant, secretary and housekeeper, he became indispensable.

The other young man who accompanied the Okamotos was Dr. Nita, a surgeon whom Kanoko had met at Keio Hospital. She had had minor surgery, and when she awoke from the anesthesia she saw the young doctor's thin face. She fell in love with him. She made no effort to hide her feelings, and this created quite a scandal among the hospital personnel. Returning home from the hospital she appealed to Ippei, like a little girl to her father, that she could not live without the beautiful young doctor.

Ippei invited Nita to visit them, but for a long time the doctor declined all invitations. When at last he visited the Okamotos—in a carriage sent by Ippei—he did not return to his dormitory room at the university. Appalled, the administration decided to transfer Nita to a small hospital in

Sapporo, a city in Hokkaido Island. Before leaving, he asked Ippei to divorce Kanoko so he could marry her and take her with him to Sapporo. It did not matter to Nita that Kanoko was twelve years his senior.

In what must have been a dramatic confrontation, Ippei confessed that, although he and Kanoko had not been living together as husband and wife in the usual sense, she was the very foundation of his life, that he could not survive without her. The three of them could go on as they had been, but Nita should not deprive him of the privilege of having Kanoko around. Nita had to accept Ippei's plea and left for Hokkaido alone.

Kanoko wrote to Nita almost every day, but soon told Ippei that she simply had to see Nita. Ippei took her to the tip of Honshu Island, handed her a round-trip ticket and made her promise to come back.

In Sapporo, Kanoko became Mrs. Nita from Tokyo. She was well respected and liked by the people around Nita, but she felt guilty for having caused the exile of this brilliant and promising doctor, forcing him to live under trying circumstances. The feeling of guilt transformed itself into infinite proofs of love given to her young lover. After a while, though, Kanoko felt a strong urge to return to Tokyo, the stage where she created and expressed herself. This pattern repeated itself often in the three years Nita was in Hokkaido.

When he finally returned to Tokyo, Nita was welcomed as a member of the family by the Okamotos. Their son Taro was away at boarding school, but Yasuo was there, studying the ancient history of Egypt at the graduate school of Keio University. There was now a strange but harmonious commune of three men and one woman in the Okamoto household.

The Nitas were one of the oldest families in the Shirakawa district of Shinshu. For many generations they had served their feudal lord as medical consultants. Nita's father had great expectations for his skilled surgeon son. When the rumor reached the village that his son was living with a much older married woman, he blamed his wife for raising a son without a backbone, a weakling, and bringing corrupt genes into his family pool. He told her to go to Tokyo and immediately bring back the errant son; otherwise he would have to divorce her since she had disgraced his family name.

The wife hurried to Tokyo to visit the Okamotos. Kanoko saw her alone first. The young doctor waited anxiously in another room. An hour later, when he was called in, he found the two woman talking and laughing together like old friends, much to his surprise.

Later, alone with her son, Mrs. Nita told him that she liked Kanoko very much. She had never met anyone like her. She was like the sun—so radiant, so bright, so merry—and she wanted to know if he was happy there with Kanoko. He was the happiest young man in the world, Nita replied, and also the most sincere since he was living out what his heart desired, with his only love.

That night, staying at the Okamotos, Mrs. Nita wrote a letter to her husband. She told him that her son was living an intense and fruitful life with a family whose center was this wonderful woman artist, and if he was still upset at his wife's inability to protect his family name, there was nothing she could do but accept the proposed divorce. Alarmed, her husband gave up the idea of rescuing his son for the time being and asked his wife to return home immediately. Mrs. Nita became so fond of Kanoko that for many years she continued to send her exquisite gifts, hand-embroidered kimonos and tortoise-shell hair ornaments.

The Okamotos arrived in London in January 1930 and took up residence in Hampstead. The official purpose of their European trip, of course, had been the Disarmament Conference, but their plans also provided that Yasuo would study history at London University, Nita would pursue medicine in Berlin, and Taro, their son, who had just begun his first year at the Art College of Tokyo, would make the indispensable visit to Paris which for so many years, had remained Kanoko's dream city.

In London, Kanoko became a special guest of the PEN

club. In the drawing room of Mrs. D. Scott she met John Galsworthy. When her hostess mentioned to Galsworthy, somewhat apologetically, that she was sorry Kanoko had come in a Western-style cocktail dress, not one of her beautiful kimonos, Galsworthy said: "Madam is an artist, so she can wear what she likes." After this, they often enjoyed afternoon teas together. In June, Kanoko went to Ireland and visited Lady Gregory at her estate in Gort. Kanoko had long admired her play, *The Rising of the Moon*.

After a year's stay in London the Okamotos left for Paris in November 1931. The city fulfilled all of Kanoko's expectations and she plunged with exuberance into a world of theaters, museums, cathedrals, cafes and restaurants. Her son Taro stayed in Paris when they went on to Germany, Italy and the United States. Kanoko never saw him again, though they carried on a correspondence until her death. These letters, which were eventually published, present a remarkable record of spiritual communication between a mother and her son.

The Okamotos returned to Japan in June 1932, and settled again in Tokyo, where Kanoko busily engaged herself with writing essays about her journey, about Buddhism and with delivering lectures. The two and a half years abroad had been extremely enjoyable and stimulating for Kanoko, and she had acquired and stored an enormous amount of creative energy.

Finally the time seemed ripe for her to begin writing fiction. In a span of less than three years, from 1936 to early 1939, she published more than twenty stories and novellas, and she left numerous manuscripts from which her husband released two novels and several stories.

Yasuo meanwhile left the Okamotos. He married and went back to the Tottori Prefecture, where he became very respected in his hometown and served as governor for two terms.

In 1937, when she was asked to contribute to an exhibition of brush-written copies of old Buddhist scrolls, Kanoko, though by then already suffering from a heart condition, worked continuously for three days and nights to complete on time a scroll that contained some twenty-five hundred Chinese characters.

On December 28, 1938, Ippei and Nita received a telephone call from an inn at Aburatsubo, a resort near Tokyo, that Kanoko had suffered a stroke and could not be moved.

Because of her health, Kanoko had not left their home alone for some time, but on that day she insisted she wanted to go out by herself. The proprietor of the inn recalled that Kanoko had been accompanied by a handsome young man who might have been a university student, but the young man disappeared before Ippei arrived at the inn, and no one knew who he was.

Kanoko Okamoto died on February 18, 1939.

Kazuko Sugisaki
translator

Notes:

1. Kanoko Okamoto's Tankas, translated from the originals by the author, are taken from *Kanoko Tanka Zenshu* (Tokyo: Shonan Shobo, 1943)

2. Letter to Shosen Ohnuki, 1911, cited in *The Collected Works of Kanoko Okamoto* (18 vols., Tokyo: Toju-sha, 1974-78)

3. Taro Okamoto, *Haha Kanoko no Omoide* (in *The Collected Works*, op cit.)

4. *Tan I Sho* (*A Lament of Discrepancies about Shinran's Teachings: Records of Shinran's Words*). Reprinted and edited by Hiroshi Noma (Tokyo: Chikuma Shobo, 1969, p. 26)

5. Kanoko Okamoto, in her preface to *Sange Sho*, 1929. (Reprint: Tokyo: Daito Shuppan Sha, 1941)

SUSHI
(Sushi)

IN THE CITY of Tokyo, one occasionally comes upon sections where downtown meets the residential area. Leaving the bustling, gay boulevards and entering suddenly into these quiet sections, one has a feeling of coming into a totally different world. Those who have become tired of the excitement of new, wide boulevards find a welcome change of mood in streets like these.

Fukuzushi, a small sushi restaurant, is located at the bottom of a hill on one of these streets. The building is not new, but the front part of the two-story house was remodeled, and copper was used for the facade. The rear of the house which is the living quarters of the family remains old except for a few new supporting poles on the steep hillside.

The restaurant has been there for some time, but the previous owner could not make a go of the business and sold it to Tomoyo's father, name and all. The new owner seemed to know how to run the place, and the small business has become prosperous.

Tomoyo's father is an excellent chef who has apprenticed in one of Tokyo's top-class restaurants and knows just what quality of sushi will suit his customers. The previous owner mainly depended on delivery service for his business, but after Tomoyo's father took it over, customers began to come into the shop to sit at the counter or small tables. At first the shop was run by only three family members, but soon it became so busy that the owner had to hire a chef, an apprentice boy and a waitress.

The customers were all different from each other, but they had one thing in common. They were all hard-pressed people caught up in the reality of everyday living, yet they wanted to get away from that reality, if only for one brief moment, to breathe fresh air. When they sat at the bar and ordered sushi, they could have it prepared exactly in the way they wanted. This was a luxury for them, not on a grand scale but a luxury all the same. Besides, while they were here they could be silly as much as they wanted. They could wear a mask, if they wished, or expose their naked self. If one said something very foolish, no one would put him down for that. The customers watched each other pick up a piece of sushi or a tea cup with a kind of intimate warmth in their eyes, as though they had been playmates of a hide-and-seek game, hiding from harsh reality.

Sushi can create a unique atmosphere, an atmosphere of diligence, speed and warm heartedness. People can indulge in this atmosphere as much as they want without spoiling it. The air carries away lightly and fluidly everything that happens in it.

The patrons of Fukuzushi were diverse: A man who used to own a gunshop, a sales manager of a department store, a dentist, a young son at a *tatami* shop, a broker who sold telephone bonds, an engineer who designed plaster casts, a toy salesman, a man promoting rabbit meat, an old retired stockbroker, and a man who, they supposed, was in show business, and did some side jobs when not appearing in the theater. He came in his oil-stained silk kimono and ate sushi picking pieces deftly with his pale fingers.

The neighboring patrons usually came to the restaurant on their way to or from, say, the barber shop. Customers who come into this area on business also dropped by. Though it varied with the season, when the days were longer, the shop was busy from four in the afternoon until the time houses began to light their lamps.

Each customer sat at his usual favorite seat. Some enjoyed *sake* with *sashimi* or vinegar-seasoned salad as hors d'oeuvre. Others would start sushi right away.

Sometimes Tomoyo's father would come out carrying a large plate from his place behind the bar. This afternoon customers saw some darkish-colored sliced fish pressed on sushi rice. The owner put the plate at the center of the table.

"What is this?" one asked.

"Well, try and see yourself. Something I enjoy with my nightcap."

The owner talked to his patrons as if they were his good friends.

"It tastes too rich for dotted shad," said the one who ate a piece first.

"Could it be Spanish mackerel?"

Someone laughed. It was Tomoyo's mother sitting by the corner post of the raised *tatami* room. She was laughing, shaking her plump body. "You people are being tricked by Father."

The fish slices were actually inexpensive salted saury. He kept it in bean curd remains for some time to remove excessive salt and oil.

"Aren't you cunning! You make such delicious sushi and enjoy it all by yourself?"

"Is this really salted saury? It tastes quite different."

The conversation was animated.

"You see, I cannot afford expensive fish for myself," said the owner.

"Why don't you add this to the menu?"

"You've got to be kidding! If I did, nobody would order expensive sushi. I can't make money on this cheap stuff."

"So, you know your business."

An unusual dish like this was occasionally served to his steady customers. A dish could be the white roe of red snapper, intestines of abalone, or the bony part of bonito left after the good filet had been sliced out. If Tomoyo, their daughter, saw these dishes, she would frown and say, "Oh, I'm tired of these. They taste so awful."

These Fukuzushi specials came out when least expected. The owner totally ignored the customer's requests, and served them simply following his whims. The customers learned not to push, because they were aware that the owner was indeed rather whimsical and stubborn about his specials. But when they really craved for one of these, they whispered it to Tomoyo, and she grudgingly found it for them.

Tomoyo grew up watching these customers. This gave her a notion that the life around her was not to be taken too seriously; it is something playful, moderate and easygoing.

When she was going to high school, she felt ashamed that she was a daughter of a small sushi shop, and took great care so that none of her classmates saw her go in and out of her home. This was not easy, and at times could be nerve-racking. Perhaps this experience gave Tomoyo a feeling of isolation, but that feeling also came from watching her parent's relationship over the years.

Her parents never quarreled, but Tomoyo felt that their hearts were completely independent of each other. They lived together out of necessity to survive in this world. Yet the way they worked together and took care of each other was more instinctive than businesslike. They did it so quietly and masterfully as if reflecting the other's wishes that they presented the image of a couple who were taciturn but compatible. The husband had a hobby of caring for little birds, which he enjoyed very much, while nourishing an ambition that someday he would open a new branch in one of those downtown high-rise buildings. The wife neither took pleasure trips nor bought new kimonos for herself. Instead, she was saving money of her own from the shop's profits. But they shared one interest in common: their daughter. They agreed that Tomoyo should receive a good education. Because society now placed more emphasis on intellectual values, they felt that their daughter should not be left behind.

I am only a chef. But my daughter should become something more than I am, the father thought. But as to how much more, the parents had no definite ideas.

Tomoyo seemed to be well acquainted with things going on around her, but her knowledge was only superficial. She was still an inexperienced young woman, happy but lonely. No one could really dislike a girl like this. But at one time her high school teachers were puzzled and alarmed when they discovered that Tomoyo was very frank with men and not shy at all. This was unusual for a girl of her age. After they were told, however, that it was part of her upbringing as a daughter of a sushi chef who needed her help in the shop, they understood and accepted her as she was.

One day a school excursion took Tomoyo to the bank of the Tama River. It was early spring. She looked into a little pool of water by the bank where the flow of the river almost stopped. The pool appeared an intense light green like the color of new tea leaves. Several silver crucian carp came floating into the pool waving their tails and feeding on the green moss of a pole. They stayed there for a short while and swam away. Quickly another group came into the pool reflecting the sun on their tail fins and were gone again. The same fish did not stay in the pool long, but the change was so swift and quiet that it seemed unnoticeable. These small carp in the pool might as well be always the same ones, she thought. Sometimes idle catfish came to join them.

Our customers are like this, Tomoyo pondered. Fukuzushi had a group of steady patrons but their members were constantly changing. And she felt she was like the green moss on the pole. The customers came and went, comforted by just touching her lightly.

Tomoyo never thought of her work at the shop as a duty. Wearing a cashmere high school uniform that hid the shape of her breasts and hips, and dragging old, clip-clap men's wooden sandals, she carried heavy cups of hot green tea to the tables. When someone teased her, hinting his interest in her as a woman, she would pout her lips, shrug her shoulder, and say, "I don't know. . . I can't answer that." Yet in her voice there was a very slight but undeniable nuance of coquetry. Then the customer would laugh, feeling something warm had touched his heart. So, in a way, Tomoyo was the Fikuzushi's drawing card.

Among the patrons was Mr. Minato, a middle-aged gentleman. He had a hint of loneliness about his eyebrows which cast a shadow over his face. He could be about fifty, but at times he looked much older. And yet, there were other times he could look like a young man with warm and passionate feelings. He had a rather stern face, but that face was softened and illumined by a sort of resignation with which he regarded the world. That sense of resignation added something clear to his personality.

He had thick, curly hair which he parted nicely, and he had a French-style mustache. Mostly he wore a homespun jacket. His pair of red shoes were often covered with dust. But occasionally he came in a striped silk kimono of good quality.

He was certainly a bachelor. But nobody knew what he did for a living. At Fukuzushi everybody called him *Sensei*, that meant a teacher or a master. From the way he ordered sushi, one knew that he was a connoisseur. But he never tried to show off his knowledge.

When he came in, he would tap the floor with his cane a few times and sit down on a stool at the bar. Leaning over the counter, he examined the fishes prepared in the glass case for the day.

"I see you have lots of variety today," he said and received a teacup from Tomoyo.

"The yellowtail has good fat in it, and also the clams are good and fresh," Tomoyo's father responded.

When Minato came in, the owner, without realizing it perhaps, would begin to wipe off the cutting board and the lacquered surface of the serving board with a clean cotton cloth. He had learned that *Sensei* was fastidious.

"Good, then I'll begin with those."

"Yes, sir!"

The owner spoke to Minato in a more polite way than to other customers. By now he remembered the course of sushi Minato usually followed. It began with *chutoto* which is the part of tuna that has a little more fat in it, then went to broiled fish garnished with thickened soy sauce. Fish with blue skin that has a light taste followed next, and ended with egg custard and a seaweed roll. To this course the chef would mix Minato's special orders for the day.

Between eating sushi and drinking tea, Minato held his hand on his cheek or rested his chin on the back of his hands folded over the head of his cane. Posing like this he could cast a fixed gaze through the house where all the screens were open, toward a pond of water half hidden by green leaves. Or the object of his gaze could be the thick oak leaves that covered the wall across the street sprinkled with cool water.

Tomoyo felt uneasy with Minato at first. But as she watched him gaze absentmindedly only at those places and pay no attention to her during the entire sushi course, even when she brought him tea, she began to feel a little disappointed. On the other hand, if their eyes happened to meet and stay locked, Tomoyo was afraid that her strength might be drawn out of her by his stare.

Tomoyo liked it best when their eyes met as if by chance only for a moment and she found him smiling at her. At these times she received certain emotional vibrations from this elderly customer. Unlike what she felt from her parents, these vibrations were vague but warm, and seemed to gently help dissolve her tension. So when Minato ignored her, Tomoyo, who might be sitting at the corner of the shop by the water heater and working on her needlepoint, stopped her hand and made a deliberate noise or tried to fake a cough or two. Though she was not aware of it, she did this to draw Minato's attention to her. Startled, Minato looked toward her, then his lips stretched smoothly over well-occluded teeth and formed a pleasant smile. One tip of his mustache went up a little as he raised his eyes. The chef, busily working with his hands, threw a glance towards Tomoyo, and realizing it was only her little tricks, kept on making sushi with his sullen face unchanged.

Minato talked with other patrons openly and he got along well with them. They talked about horse races, the stock market, politics, the games of *go* and chess, and bonsai. These were the common subjects among people who gathered in small restaurants. Minato joined the conversation but let others do most of the talking. Yet that did not give the impression he looked down upon them or he was bored with them. His manners proved otherwise.

For instance, when he was offered a cup of *sake*, he received it in his firm and slender hand, gesturing with it to show how much he appreciated it.

"Actually my doctor told me I shouldn't drink, but since you are so kind to offer me, well, I shall gladly accept it."

From the way he emptied the cup, one could see that he thoroughly enjoyed it. Then he returned the emptied cup to the customer and, deftly lifting a small porcelain bottle, poured *sake* into it. One could make no mistake from Minato's attitude on such occasions that he really enjoyed being with people. It also showed that he was that kind of person who, having received kindness, would have to return it many times over. So it was agreed among the patrons that *Sensei* was a very nice person indeed.

But Tomoyo was not particularly happy to see Minato behave like this. It was too light for his personality, she felt. He was diminishing something precious of his own by responding so heartily to anyone's whim. Why did he, who looked grim usually, have to act like an old man starving for human warmth? To Tomoyo watching him behave like this, even his ring with an ancient Egyptian scarab seemed detestable.

Once, when a customer, overjoyed by Minato's sincere response, kept on exchanging cups of *sake* with him and Minato was laughing and enjoying himself, Tomoyo stood up, walked up to them and snatched the cup from Minato's hand.

"You said your doctor didn't want you to drink. You must stop now."

She thrust back the cup to the other customer and strode away. It was not so much her concern for Minato's health that made her do it, but it was a curious jealousy she felt for him.

"I see, Tomoyo can be a good caring wife," said the other customer. People laughed and things were let go at that. Minato smiled awkwardly, bowed slightly to his company, reseated himself to face the chef, and picked up his heavy tea cup.

Lately Tomoyo found herself thinking of Minato more often. And this somehow made her behave strangely. Sometimes she ignored him completely not saying a word to him. Seeing him come into the shop, she would stand up and did not come near him. At Tomoyo's cool reception, Minato might smile light-heartedly. But when Tomoyo was not there at all, he looked lonely and gazed more intensely at the street and the green canyon at the back of the house.

One day Tomoyo took a basket and went to an insect store on the boulevard to buy singing frogs. Her father enjoyed caring for these small creatures and he was good at it. Even so, they occasionally died. It was the beginning of the summer, and the song of the frogs that invited coolness were welcome music.

As she came near the store Tomoyo saw Minato come out of it carrying a glass jar. He did not see her, and taking great care with the jar, walked slowly away from her. While the storekeeper was putting the frogs in the basket, Tomoyo went out and saw where Minato was going.

With the basket on her arm, Tomoyo hurried out to overtake Minato.

"*Sensei*! Hey, *Sensei*!" She called out to him.

"Well, well, Tomoyo, is that you? What a surprise! I never meet you outside your restaurant."

They began to walk together and showed their purchases to each other. Minato had bought several ghost fish with transparent flesh through which one could see quite clearly their skeleton and small sinuous intestines.

"Do you live around here?" Tomoyo asked.

"Yes, I live in an apartment right over there. But I don't know for how long."

Minato said he wanted to invite Tomoyo for tea. They walked about looking for a good cafe, but they could not find a place they liked.

"We cannot go to Ginza with this, can we?" Minato looked at the glass jar of ghost fish.

"No, we can't," Tomoyo said, "but we don't have to go to Ginza. We can sit down and rest maybe in a vacant lot."

Minato looked around him and seemed to notice that the season of green was now in full bloom. He exhaled a deep breath to the sky and said, "Why, that is a splendid idea."

They turned away from the wide boulevard, and soon found a vacant lot where a hospital used to stand at the edge of a cliff. The building burned down some time ago, and a half-collapsed brick wall gave the appearance of a Roman ruin. They put their purchases down, sat on the grass, and stretched their legs.

Tomoyo thought that she had had many questions she wanted to ask Minato. But now that she was with him, those questions seemed unimportant. She felt very peaceful and calm as if enveloped by a scented mist. It was Minato who was animated.

"You look very grown up today!" He was in a good mood. Tomoyo wanted to say something nice, but all she could think of was a question that did not seem to matter much."

"Do you really like sushi?"

"I'm not sure," was Minato's answer.

"Then why do you come to our shop so often?"

"I don't dislike sushi. I'm rather fond of it actually. But I go to your restaurant mainly because it comforts me to eat sushi even when I don't particularly want it."

"What do you mean?" Tomoyo wondered.

Minato began to tell Tomoyo why eating sushi, even when he had no particular craving for it, could comfort him.

"It may be true that a strange child is born into an old, decaying family. Or perhaps a child can feel more keenly than an adult a premonition that precedes the fall of the house. Or a baby could be affected by this strong premonition in his mother's womb even. . . "

With these words Minato began his story:

The child did not like anything sweet. For snacks he only ate salted rice crackers. When he ate a cracker, he brought his upper and lower teeth close together and carefully bit into its flat, round shape. If the cracker was not stale, the biting made a nice crunching sound. The child chewed the piece in his mouth carefully and thoroughly and swallowed it. Now he was ready for the second bite. Again he brought his upper and lower teeth close together and between them he put the edge of the cracker. When he bit, he closed his eyes so that he could listen to the sound better.

"Crunch!"

He knew that there were many different tones in the same "crunch" sound. When his teeth made the tone he liked best, he was so happy that his whole body shook with joy. He paused a while, thinking, his eyes moist with tears.

The child lived with his parents, a brother and a sister, both were older than he was. There were maids, too. But the whole family considered him odd. His eating habit was very peculiar. He disliked fish. He could eat only a few kinds of vegetables, and absolutely no meat.

It was partly the change of the time that caused the old house to fall, but also it was the father's character that contributed more to the tragedy. He preferred to put on an air of grandiosity, hiding timidity inside, and saying, "No, no, no need to worry, we still have lots of money."

The father putting on an easy air came occasionally to check on what the child was eating.

"How is the boy doing? Is he eating well enough to survive?" he would ask his wife.

On the boy's small table were plain scrambled eggs and some dried seaweed. The mother tried to shield the plate with her kimono sleeve from her husband's prying eyes, and said, "Please don't make a fuss about it. If you do, he won't eat even these because he is very bashful."

It was actually painful for the child to eat. He felt the lumps of food with their color, smell and taste would contaminate his body. He wished for food as pure as air. When he had nothing in his stomach he did feel hungry, yet he was afraid to eat. He put his cheek on a cold marble art object placed in the alcove and licked it. He felt he was fainting, with his head cool and very clear. If it was just when the sun was setting behind the hill beyond the little pond in the valley (the geography of the child's neighborhood was much like that of Fukuzushi's), the boy felt he did not mind fainting, nor even dying. But instead of letting go, he did something else. He put his hands under the *obi* sash tied tightly around his empty stomach and, bending forward with his face up-turned, he called out, "Mother!"

But he was not calling his own mother. He liked his mother best of all in the family yet he had the feeling that some-where else there was a woman he could really call his "Mother." Of course, if that woman could have heard his call and appeared to him, he might have fainted. Even so there was some sad comfort in calling to this woman.

"Mother, Mother. . . ."

He kept calling in a voice thick like paper trembling in the wind.

"Yes, dear, did you call me?" Answering, his mother came to him. "Oh, poor child, what's the matter with you? What are you doing here?'

She grabbed his shoulder and shook him. She looked into his eyes. He was embarrassed by the mistake this mother made, and blushed a little.

"This is why I want you to eat. I really wish you would eat three good meals a day. Please, would you do that for me?"

Her voice was shaking. After a great deal of anxiety and trial and error, the mother found out that the only foods the child could take were eggs and dried seaweed.

He could swallow them because, even though they made his stomach heavy, he felt they did not taint his body. There were times when he felt some sad and lonely feeling fill his entire body. Then he would bite into anything sour and soft. So he went out to pick green plums and small unripe tangerines. During the rainy season of May, the child knew as well as a bird where to find these fruit trees in the hills and valleys of the city.

The boy did well at school. He had a photographic memory and could remember anything he read or heard once. But he was bored with lessons that were so easy. The boredom made him standoffish and this attitude strangely contributed to his excellent academic achievement.

At school as well as at home, everybody treated him differently.

One day his parents were quarreling bitterly behind the closed door. The mother came out and took the boy aside. She was very serious, and said to him:

"Now listen to me carefully, my dear. Your teachers are very much concerned about you because you are so thin and still losing weight. They think that we are not paying proper attention to your health at home. Your father has heard of this, and. . . you know how he is, he blames me for everything."

The mother sat down in front of the boy, and putting her palms flat on the *tatami* floor, bowed to him. "Please, I beg you, dear, please try to eat more so that you'll gain weight and become healthier. Otherwise, I don't think I can stay here. I feel I have no place in this house."

I have committed the sin, the boy thought, the sin he had known his ill-formed character was bound to commit someday. He had caused his own mother to bow to him, with her hands flat on the floor. His face flushed and his body began to shake. But he felt a strange peace inside. He thought to himself, I have done something very wrong, so wrong that I might as well be dead. I don't care if I die. I'll eat anything. If eating something strange should make me vomit, make my body impure and rot, so be it. I won't regret it. Maybe it's better that I am dead, because as long as I am alive, I'll be so choosy about what I can or cannot eat, and that will make me a big trouble to everybody around me, and to myself, as well.

So the boy sat down at the regular family dinner table and pretending that he could handle anything now, he began to eat. He ate a mouthful, and he vomited. He had tried hard to make his tongue and throat numb so that he wouldn't taste anything. But as soon as he swallowed, the thought that the food he had just eaten was prepared by women other than his mother wrenched his stomach. The image of the maid's red underwear flashing through her kimono and that of the darkish hair oil dripping down the side of an old woman who cooked rice rummaged through his stomach.

His brother and sister looked at him with disgust. The father merely glanced at him out of the corner of his eye and kept on emptying his *sake* cup. The mother cleaned up the mess in a hurry. She looked at her husband's face reproachfully and sighed.

"You see, it's not only my fault. He is like this."

But still she acted timidly toward her husband.

The next day the mother brought out a new thin *tatami* mat and spread it in the corridor where the young leaves of the garden cast green shadows. She also had a cutting board, a knife, a wooden bowl and a miniature screened cupboard. They were all new, she had just bought them herself. The mother made the boy sit on the other side of the cutting

board. She set a small table in front of him and put a plate
on it.

She tucked her sleeves up high, stretched her arms toward him and flipping her hands many times like a magician showed him her clean rosy palms. Rubbing her palms
together with a rhythm, she said, "Now watch this. Everything I have here is new and clean. The cook is your mother.
My hands have been scrubbed and washed. Did you see it?
Yes you did, didn't you? Now then, let me see . . . ."

In the wooden bowl, the mother mixed sweet vinegar with
warm rice. Both of them coughed a little because of the sour
steam evaporating from the bowl. The mother drew the bowl
to her side, took out a small handful of rice from it, and
made it into an oval shape. In the screened cupboard, various sushi ingredients had been neatly prepared on a plate.
She took one piece, quickly put it on the rice ball, pressed it
lightly, and placed it on the boy's plate. It was a sliced piece
of egg custard.

"There, it's sushi, you can eat sushi with your hand."

As the mother told him, the boy picked it up with his
fingers and ate it. The taste of vinegar-seasoned warm rice
mixed gently with sweet egg custard spread on his tongue.
It was delicious. It gave him the feeling that his naked skin
was caressed with soft smooth hands. Savoring, he swallowed it. Then he felt a strange sensation: this delicious taste

of sushi mingling with his love for the mother suddenly sprung in himself like warm scented water, and filled his entire body.

The boy was too shy to say he liked it. So he just grinned awkwardly and looked up at his mother's face.

"Would you like another one?"

The mother again flipped her hands over a few times like a magician, took out one slice from the cupboard, pressed it on a rice ball, and put it on his plate.

The boy looked at the small white rectangular slice on the rice. He felt revolted. The mother saw it, and with an air of authority that wasn't too frightening, said to him, "It's nothing to be afraid of. Just think of it as white egg custard."

This was the first time that the boy had eaten a slice of squid. It was as smooth as ivory and easier to chew than the white rice cake just pounded. In the middle of this great adventure of chewing squid, he let out a deep breath shut up so long in him. Then he felt his face muscles really relaxed. He did not say he liked it. He only smiled to his mother.

For the next sushi the mother used a piece of transparent fish. As he picked it up its fishy smell frightened him a little. He held his breath to block the smell, and encouraging himself to be brave, put it in his mouth. The white transparent piece surprised him with its wonderful taste. The more he

chewed it, the more delicious it became on his tongue and
he could feel its nutrition passing through his thin throat,
coming into his body.

It must have been a real fish, he knew. He could actually
eat fish! For the first time in his life he felt a new strength
being born in him. It was a fresh power of a conqueror who
had just killed a live animal by biting into it, tearing it. He
was so happy that he looked around as far as he could. This
happiness made the sides of his belly itch, and he raised his
dancing fingers to scratch them.

"Hee, hee, hee. . . ," the child laughed a strange high-
pitched laugh.

The mother knew that victory was hers now. She picked
grains of rice off her hands slowly, one by one, and with a
deliberate calmness looked into the screened cupboard.

"What shall I make next? Let me see, is anything left in
here?"

The child could hardly wait for the next sushi. He was
screaming now, "Sushi! Sushi!"

The mother hid her joy and kept a vacant expression on
her face. It was the beautiful face that the boy liked best of
all, the face he had never forgotten all his life.

"Well then, since my customer requests it, I shall make
another sushi for him."

She again stretched her rosy hands toward him, and flipped them over like a magician, and made another piece. It had a slice of white fish like the one before. The mother had chosen the kind of fish with very little color and smell for this first venture. They were flounder and red snapper slices.

The boy kept eating one after another. The mother and the child were racing now. As soon as the mother had made one sushi and put it on his plate, the boy picked it up. They were so engrossed in the race and being drawn together into a passionate numbness that they thought of nothing else. A delightful rhythm accompanied their hands. The mother could not make all the pieces in a neat even shape like a professional chef. Sometimes a slice of fish rolled sideways and dropped on the plate. The boy loved it even more when this happened. He picked up the fish, put it on the rice ball and rearranged the shape before he ate it. It tasted better if he did this.

The image of the phantom mother he had been secretly calling and this mother who was making sushi for him now became superimposed, became almost one. Was it happening in his imagination, or was it an optical illusion, he wondered. He wanted the two to become one, of course; but if that happened, he would have been frightened. Could it be possible that the phantom mother was the same as this mother who was giving him such delicious food? If so, he was sorry, very sorry, that he directed his love to another woman, betraying this mother.

"That should be enough for today. Thank you, dear, I'm glad you ate so well!"

The mother sitting before him clapped her hands looking very satisfied.

After the first success the mother did this several times, and the child grew accustomed to her own homemade sushi. He could eat now red clams which looked like a pomegranate flower and a half-beak, a small slender fish with two silver lines on its back. Gradually he was getting used to other fish served at the family dinner table. His health improved astonishingly. By the time he was in high school, he was a magnificently beautiful young man whom people would turn around to admire.

All of a sudden his father who had been standoffish and cold toward the son took an interest in him. He made the boy sit at the dinner table with him and they drank *sake* together. He took him to a billiard hall and to restaurants where geishas came to entertain them.

And their old house was gradually falling. But the father ignored the grim fact, and took pleasure watching his beautiful son in a blue indigo kimono drink *sake* from a small cup. He was proud to see other women make much fuss about him. At sixteen the son was already an accomplished playboy.

The mother who had raised the son with such love and efforts accused her husband furiously.

"You have corrupted him! You have thoroughly corrupted my son!"

To her desperate fury the father responded only with his wry smile. The son could not help feeling disgust for the parents who quarreled bitterly as if to bury in the quarrel the oppressive fact of the decaying house.

At school, lessons were almost too easy for him. Without studying at home, he stayed at the top of his class. He had no difficulty entering one of the best universities in Tokyo. Even so he could not shake off a kind of sad emptiness, a void he did not know how to fill. But he seemed to understand that he would not be able to fill this emptiness quickly. In a long period of melancholy and boredom he graduated from the university and found himself a job.

The house had fallen completely. Both parents died, and soon after that, his brother and sister followed them. The son, who was capable enough, was given an important position at any workplace he chose. But somehow he could not interest himself in staying there and climbing up the corporate ladder.

His second wife died when he was about fifty. Around that time he had a lucky break in the stock market and acquired enough money to live comfortably for the rest of his life. So he left the job and quit working. He gave up his home, too. Since then he has been moving from one apartment to another, not wanting to settle down in one place.

"I am the child and the young man in this story," Minato told Tomoyo when he finished.

"Now I see why you like sushi so much," Tomoyo responded.

"Well, actually, after I grew up, I didn't enjoy it so much as I used to. But lately memories of my mother come back to me very often. It may be that I myself am getting old. I miss her very much, and when I think of her, I also miss sushi."

A wisteria arbor grew from the ground near the remains of the burned hospital. Supporting poles had collapsed and the twisted vines of the tree hung down to the ground. Yet young leaves sprouted from the tip of the vines, and the cluster of thin flowers bloomed looking like drops of purple dew. An azalea bush remained. It used to decorate the base of a rock in the garden. The rock was carried away leaving a hole in the ground. The plant, with one side burned, still had white flowers.

The edge of the garden dropped down steeply, and the streetcar rail ran at the bottom. The noise of the streetcar shook the air from time to time. Purple wall irises among Japanese snake beards were swinging in the evening breeze. The shadow of a fat palm trunk became slantingly long and dark on the grass. They were in the shadow now. The singing frogs in Tomoyo's basket sang a song or two. They smiled at it, at each other.

"It's getting late. You want to go home now," Minato said to Tomoyo.

Tomoyo stood up with the basket on her arm. Minato lifted the glass jar of ghost fish and gave it to Tomoyo. Then he went home.

After that day, Minato did not come back to Fukuzushi.

"What has happened to *Sensei* these days? We haven't seen him for some time. Does anyone know?"

Patrons asked among themselves. But soon they forgot about him.

Tomoyo didn't know how to find him. She wished she had asked where he lived. Often she went to the vacant lot in which they sat that afternoon and just stood there, or sat on a rock remembering Minato. Then tears came into her eyes. But after a while she would walk home, slowly, absentmindedly. Time went by, and Tomoyo visited the lot less and less, and finally, not at all.

When she remembers Minato now, she simply tells herself:

Sensei must have moved again, and must be going to another sushi shop. After all, there is always a sushi restaurant in any neighborhood.

Her memory of Minato is already fading.

1939

THE OLD GEISHA
(Rogi Sho)

H ER REAL NAME is Sonoko Hiraide, but it does not fit her personality just as the real name of a Kabuki actor does not fit. But if we call her by her professional name, Kosono, it also doesn't do justice to the dignified grace she has begun to acquire these days as she is gradually trying to give up her profession. So, it is better to call her here simply "old geisha."

Often people see her in a department store in the middle of the day. Her hairdo is an ordinary western style, and she wears her twilled silk kimono like a respectable non-professional woman. In this style, she walks about with a melancholy expression on her face followed by a young maid.

Many times she walks around the same section of the store, dangling her two arms down along her stout body and kicking out her legs at each step.

Or she speeds fast and straight as the thread of a kite, then stops unexpectedly at a farther counter. But she doesn't seem to be aware of anything except the loneliness of the middle of the day. If her bluish oval eyes happen to catch something of interest, they slowly open and focus on the object as though she were looking at a peony flower in her dream. Her lips twist as they did when she was a young girl and break into a smile for a moment, but soon the melancholy expression returns to her face.

It is an entirely different story with her, however, at the place of her profession. If she meets a good rival there, she is quiet at first with a blank look on her face, then she begins to speak fluently, and that talk can last for a long time.

When the former mistress of Shinkiraku Restaurant was still alive, she was a good rival of the old geisha. And there was another one, the owner of Hisago of Shinbashi. When the three of them got together they could carry on a very witty and animated conversation typical of their profession. When this happened even well-experienced geishas would leave their customers and gather around them wanting to learn the skill of conversation. The old geisha might talk about her experiences even without these rivals if she had the audience of her favorite young ones.

Once, when she was only an apprentice, the old geisha would begin, she laughed so much at the erotic, frank talk exchanged between her elder "sisters" and their customers that she found herself wetting the *tatami* floor. She was so embarrassed that she could not stand up and began crying. Or when she was a kept woman, the geisha began another story, she eloped with a young lover and the patron took her mother as a hostage. After she established herself as the owner of a geisha house, once she was so hard-pressed financially that she was forced to hire a carriage that cost her twelve yen at the end of the month to get a five yen loan she needed immediately.

Her stories were endless, and they made the young geishas laugh so much, almost to the point of exhaustion. Though their contents were more or less the same always, her storytelling technique made them hilariously funny each time. It was as though the old geisha had been possessed and pursued her young listeners with her sharpened enchanting nails, trying to thrust them into their flesh. Envious of youth, old age seemed to cunningly torture the young.

The young geishas, their hair now disheveled, held their sides and gasped, "Oh, please stop, stop now! We'll die, if you keep on."

Kosono never gossiped about the people still alive, but her observations of those now dead with whom she had had some relationships were unique and penetrating. There were, unexpectedly, well-known artists and other celebrities among them.

There was a familiar episode about the geisha, though it might not be true. When the famous Chinese actor, Mei Lang-fang, came to Tokyo to appear in the Imperial Theater, she went to the wealthy promoter who brought the actor from China, and begged him, "Please let me meet the actor in private. I don't care how much money it takes."

But the promoter somehow managed to persuade her not to pursue the idea, and sent her home.

One of the young listeners, to avenge the pain of her laughing, asked her, panting for breath:

"Is it true that you took out your bank book from the fold of your obiage sash and showed it to the promoter to prove you have enough money?"

"What nonsense! Did you say *obiage*? I wasn't a child any more. I didn't need a scarf-like *obiage* to tie my *obi*."

She was angry like a child. This child-like anger coming from the mature geisha was very amusing to watch. So, the young ones often brought up the subject just to enjoy it.

"But you see," the old geisha would say after her long talk, "looking back, I know now that what I have been doing is to find one man among all those men I had in my life. I was attracted to this part of this man, or that part of another. But those were only parts of the ideal man that I have been looking for. That's why I couldn't have a lasting relationship with any one of them."

"And who could be that ideal man? Did you find out?" asked a young girl.

"If I did, my troubles would be over forever. Who knows, it might have been my first love, or I may still meet him someday."

When Kosono said this, her face had that melancholic expression which she seldom showed in her professional life.

"In a way I envy an ordinary housewife. All she has to do is to stay faithful with the husband her parents choose for her. She knows only one man in her life, has children by him, and in her old age, she is taken care of by these children. No worries, no doubts whatsoever."

When the old geisha's talk came to this point, the young ones would whisper among themselves that though they enjoyed listening to her, they were not too happy about her depressing tone at the end.

In the last ten years, after Kosono became comfortably well off and rather free to choose which parties she entertained, she had come to prefer a healthy middle-class lifestyle to her professional one. She had divided her house into two separate sections: one was the geisha house quarter, and the other, her living area, to which a storehouse with traditional whitewashed walls was connected. She built an independent entrance to the living section facing a narrow back street. The entrance suggested the house to be a home with no relation to the front geisha quarter. Kosono also adopted a girl from a distant relative and sent her to high school. She took up lessons that were more modern and intellectual than those of traditional geisha training.

The old geisha was introduced to me by a mutual acquaintance who lived in downtown Tokyo, for lessons of *tanka*, a traditional short poem with thirty-one syllables. At our first meeting she said something like this:

"A geisha is like a multi-purpose knife. It doesn't have to be very sharp to cut one particular thing, but it has to cut any number of things. I want to learn *tanka* just enough to please more sophisticated customers now that I entertain them often."

For about a year I gave her lessons. Then, I discovered that although she had nice feelings for this form of poem, her talent suited haiku more. So I asked a woman haiku poet I knew to take her as her student. After she left me, she sent her gardener to build a small pond and a fountain in the old town Tokyo style in my inner garden, to show her gratitude.

The old geisha had her main living quarters remodeled in half-western style and installed various electric devices. What had motivated this was her nature that always wanted the best. She saw them in a newly built restaurant where she entertained customers, and she wanted the same things for her home. After they were installed, she realized that in the way these devices worked there was something healthy and mysterious: an instant water heater that streamed out hot water as soon as she poured cold water into it, an ashtray with an electric lighter which, pushed down with the tip of her long pipe, instantly lighted tobacco for her. She felt a fresh thrill she'd never known before in using them.

"They seem to be alive. . . un huh. . . well, everything should work as well as these," she said.

The world of speed and exactness is what she learned from electric devices. Standing on this vantage point she could look back on her life now. In the world I have been living in, things went so slow and inefficiently, she thought, like turning the oil lamp on and off over and over again. For a while after she had the devices installed, the old geisha got up early in the morning and enjoyed toying with them, although she was annoyed with the big electric bill she received.

The devices broke down frequently, and Makita, the owner of a nearby electric shop, came to repair them. As he worked, the geisha followed him around and watched with curiosity. Soon she began to know a little about electricity.

"I see, when plus and minus currents meet together, they can do a lot of things, un huh. . . it's like two people being compatible," she said. Her admiration for a new civilization had increased a great deal.

Makita came often to help her since she did not have a man in her household. One day he brought along a young man, and told the geisha that this man would take care of her electric appliances from now on. Yuki was the young man's name. He was cheerful and carefree. Looking around the house he made a rude remark, "This is supposed to be a geisha house, isn't it? But you don't have a *shamisen*."

He came often. The carefree and refreshing atmosphere the young man bore about him attracted the geisha, and they came to enjoy their talks together.

"Your work, Yuki, is really clumsy. As soon as you repair something it breaks down again. It doesn't last a week."

She was talking like a man.

"If so, I can't help it. I can't feel any 'passion' for petty jobs like these."

"What did you say? What is that 'passion'?"

"'Passion' means, well. . . let me see. If I put it in your terms, it's an erotic attraction, maybe. I don't feel that for a job like this."

This made her think of her life. She remembered many parties she served, many men she slept with without being attracted to them, without feeling "passion" for them. She felt sorry for her past.

"I see. Then, tell me what kind of work can you feel passion for?"

The young man said that it would be to invent something new, and to have it patented, and to make a lot of money with it.

"Well, okay, why don't you do it, then?"

Yuki looked her in the face.

"'Why don't you do it?' Ah, la la, it's not so simple. This is why people call your kind of women playthings. You can't talk sense."

"No, you don't understand. I said it because I have already made up my mind to help you. If I take care of your living expenses, would you consider devoting yourself to what you feel passion for?"

So Yuki left Makita's store and came to live in one of the rental houses the geisha owned. With Yuki's instruction she had a room remodeled into a workshop and installed some apparatus for his research and experiments.

Yuki had worked his way through school. When he graduated from the college of electrical engineering, however, he did not find himself a full-time job. He needed time for his ambition. He worked here and there as a part-time helper, which was almost as unrewarding as day labor. Then he met Makita who came from the same hometown as Yuki.

Makita offered him a position of a live-in engineer. Yuki moved in with his family. But there were several small children in the house, and the jobs were petty and numerous. The situation was driving him almost to his wit's end. So Yuki quickly accepted the offer made by the geisha.

Yuki was not especially grateful to her, however. He figured that maybe this was the kind of thing an old geisha would do. A woman who had led a pleasure-filled life squeezing easy money out of men might do things like this to ease her guilt. Although he was not so impudent as to assume that he was doing her a favor by accepting the offer, he felt he didn't owe her much.

For the first time in his life, he did not have to worry about his daily meals. He was happy with the quiet and sincere life he was leading. He spent his day laboriously contrasting what he read in textbooks with the results of the experiments, and making notes of anything that seemed useful for a new invention. He looked at himself in the mirror. There was an image of a young man with a strong, masculine body. He liked himself. He wore a linen shirt. His hair was curled by an electric curler. The man sat slantingly on a chair smoking leisurely. It was an image most suitable for a young inventor, he acknowledged, totally different from what he used to be.

A wooden verandah surrounded his workshop, and there was a small rectangular garden beyond. A few trees grew there. When he was exhausted with his work, he went out to the verandah, lay down flat on his back, looked up at the blurred blue sky of the city, and transplanted his many fantasies into dreams.

Kosono came to visit Yuki every few days. She looked around the place, observed what was lacking, and later had them sent from her house.

"You are a young man easy to take care of. Your house looks always neat and clean. You never have dirty clothes piled up," Kosono complimented.

"Sure, it's nothing for me. My mother died young, so I changed and washed my own diapers as a baby."

"Oh no," the old geisha laughed. Then, looking sad, she said, "But I've heard that if a man is too fastidious about small things, he can't make a big success."

"Well, I don't think this is the real me either, but somehow this neatness has become my habit. So if I see untidiness about me, I feel uneasy."

"I don't know why. . . at any rate, be sure to let me know if you need anything," the geisha insisted.

On the day of *hatsuuma*, that is the first "Horse Day" of the lunar February, the geisha had *inari* sushi with fried bean curd delivered to her house, and ate it with Yuki relaxing like mother and son.

The foster daughter, Michiko, was a capricious girl. For a while she came to see Yuki everyday and wanted him to keep her company. Growing up in this special society where love is treated like a commodity, Michiko knew no other way to treat it. Kosono had tried to shield her daughter, but in vain. Michiko was precocious about love, though that was only skin deep. She had hurried through her adolescence without really experiencing it, and her child's heart seemed to have hardened as it was, acquiring a thin layer of adult discretion on its surface.

Realizing that Yuki did not enjoy spending time with her, Michiko lost her interest in him, and she did not visit him for a long time. Then one day she appeared again looking rather sluggish. Here is a young man her mother is taking care of, she reasoned, so she had better take advantage of the situation and make the best of it. Still, she was not too happy that her mother brought a total stranger into their life.

Michiko sat on Yuki's lap casually and gave him a coquettish sidelong glance that was perfect but only in form.

"Can you tell how much I weigh?"

Yuki raised his knees a few times.

"For a girl of your age, marriageable age that is, you lack delicacy of manners."

"No, that's not true. I got an A in ethics in school."

Did she misinterpret the term, "delicacy of manner" or did she choose to misinterpret?

Through her clothes Yuki's hand felt her body. He thought it was droll that this young girl whose body was like an undernourished child's was trying to imitate the coquetry of a full-grown woman. He laughed.

"Oh, how dare you laugh at me! I know you think you are so great." Michiko stood up, she was angry.

"Do some exercises and build up your body like your mother's."

After this, Michiko literally hated him, though she did not quite understand why.

Yuki's sense of happiness lasted about half a year. Then he began to feel rather uncertain about it. When he was only toying with ideas of inventions, they all seemed wonderful. But once he began research and experiments, he had to face the fact that the kind of things he had in mind had already been invented and patented. Even if he believed his versions more advanced and useful, he would have to make changes in order not to conflict with the patented products. Besides he was not sure whether the devices he was going

to create might meet much demand. He knew by now that
there had been many good inventions, admirable from the
professional point of view, but not at all used by people. On
the other hand, one casual flash of an idea could be a smash-
ing success. He had understood that inventions of new
things could be speculative, but hadn't the least idea that
there was such a taxing conflict between the imagined products and actual materialization of them.

Yet he himself was the real reason he was losing interest
in this life. He remembered those days when he had to work
on trivial jobs. He didn't like it, but he could bear it because
he had an ambition, a thrilling dream that someday he would
have enough money to devote himself to creation of new
things. But this ambition once materialized, living it daily
was boring , almost tormenting. Working in quiet isolation
he became sometimes frightened with the notion that he
might be going in an entirely wrong direction in his research,
and thus would be left behind the mainstream of the time.

Besides he was not sure if he really wanted to be rich.
Now, he did not have to earn a living anymore. If he wanted
to go out occasionally, his idea of having a good time was
limited. He would see a movie, enjoy a drink or two at a bar
and in pleasant intoxication of *sake*, take a taxi home. That
was all. And the old geisha was willing to give him enough
money to spend on this modest pleasure. It was more than

he asked for. Once or twice Yuki had gone to gay quarters with his friends. He enjoyed the woman only for the money he paid for her. As soon as he was done, he wanted to come home to relax, to stretch his body in his comfortable futon and sleep. He never stayed out all night. He had a very luxurious set of *futon*, almost too good for a young man like him. He had bought some down himself, and made his own comforters with it.

I don't seem to have any more desire than this, do I? Have I become something abnormal for a man of my age? Yuki wondered. And he was frightened to find himself strangely passive, neutralized.

What a contrast she makes! That old geisha is so different from me! What kind of woman is she, anyway. Yuki's thoughts wandered toward her. Her face always looked melancholy, yet she had something indomitable and un-yielding in her. Take her lessons, for instance, she was constantly challenging new things, as if she was trying to devour the unknown. She was being pushed forward by her satisfaction as well as her dissatisfaction.

So the next time Kosono came to his workshop, Yuki asked her, "Do you know of Mistanguette, a very famous night-club entertainer in France?"

"Yes, I've heard her songs on a record. . . . The way she sings those intricate melodies are really marvelous."

"I was told once that the old singer has all her wrinkles tucked in the sole of her feet. But I imagine you don't have to do that yet, do you?"

Her eyes glared for an instant, then with a quick smile she said, "Me? Well, I have to eat so many New Year's Eve peas now, you know you eat as many peas as your age, so I doubt if my skin will act as it used to. But let me see . . . ."

The old geisha rolled up her kimono sleeve and thrust her left arm to Yuki.

"Pinch the skin of my upper arm with your thumb and forefinger. Pinch it tight and hold it."

Yuki did as he was told. The geisha held the skin of the opposite side of the arm with her right fingers and pinched it back. The part of skin that Yuki's fingers had held slipped away gently and returned to its original smoothness. He tried it once more, harder this time, but still he could not hold the skin. The resilient smoothness like the belly skin of an eel and the mysterious whiteness resembling parchment— these sensations Yuki felt from her skin remained in him long afterward.

"How weird! But, really you are amazing!"

The old geisha rubbed off the red mark left by Yuki's fingers with the sleeve of her silk underwear, and said:

"I owe this to childhood dance training. Teachers used to strike and beat children during lessons, you know . . . ."

The memories of those hard times came back to her, casting for a moment a dark shadow on her face.

Then she said to him, "What has become of you?" And staring at him, she continued. "Don't misunderstand me. I am not saying that I want you to work harder or to become a quick success. But let's say that if you were a fish, you've lost your freshness. It's a bit strange to me that you, a young man who should have enough worries of his own, is wondering about the age of an old woman. Is your mind shrinking with a mean twist?"

"Actually, I'm getting disappointed with myself," Yuki confessed. "I'm losing passion for the world. No, that's not true, I'm not losing it. I never had it from the beginning."

"No, that's not true. You had it all right. But if that is the case, if you are losing your passion, you have a problem. I see, though, you've put on weight, and are looking much better than before."

It was true that Yuki had put on some weight and his well-built body had acquired roundness, which now gave him an air of wealth. And there was a sensuous glow in the soft swell of the eyelids above his brown eyes and the corpulent flesh under his chin.

"Yes, my health is good, so good that I feel I can doze off at any moment. And I can't remember anything these days, unless I try very hard. Even important things escape my mind. And the funny thing is that I have a kind of insecure feeling, uneasiness. I've never known anything like this before."

"Maybe you are eating too much *mugitoro*, you know, that ground white yam over the wheat and rice could give you more energy than you need."

The old geisha teased him because she knew that Yuki often had his orders of *mugitoro* delivered from a neighborhood restaurant famous for this dish. Quickly she became serious again and said, "Well, I think it won't hurt if you look for something to worry about. Find a trouble, a trouble of any kind. Sometimes you are better off with a certain amount of anxiety."

A few days after that the geisha invited him for an outing. Michiko and two young geishas from another house came along. Yuki had not met them, but they looked nice in their good kimonos. They bowed to Kosono and thanked her very politely for asking them for the outing.

The old geisha said to Yuki, "This is going to be your entertainment party. I paid these women geisha fees for a whole day. So, you are their man for today. Let them entertain you and just enjoy it."

As expected, the young geishas worked very hard to please Yuki. When they were getting into a boat at the Takeya pier, the younger one asked him, "Can you hold my hand, please? I need you."

Getting into the boat, she staggered on purpose and held on to Yuki. He could see her round nape that looked transparently white against a red silk collar. The border of the nape hair met there with the pale misty skin of her back. Yuki smelled scented hair oil, too. On her thickly made up profile, the cheeks showed an enamel-like glow and her nose cut a fine statuesque line.

"It's very beautiful out here," the old geisha remarked. Sitting on the shiftboard of the boat, she took out a tobacco case and a lighter from the fold of her *obi* sash.

They walked or rode in a taxi, admiring the early summer scenes along the Arakawa Canal. Factories were built there and homes for the factory workers were added on the cinder-paved land. But the old sections of *Kanegafuchi* and Ayase still remained here and there. Only a few silk trees that the Ayase River was known for were left. The only thing that had stayed the same was a group of boat carpenters working on a reed island beyond the stream.

"When I was living in Mukojima as a kept woman," the old geisha began to reminisce, "my patron was such a jealous man that he didn't let me go beyond this neighborhood. So I used to tell him I was only going for a short walk along the river. My young lover disguised himself as a carp fisherman and moored his boat under the row of those silk trees. That's how we did our 'rendezvous' as you people call it now, in the boat."

As the evening approached, silk tree flowers began to fold, and the sound of the boat carpenters' hammers trailed off. One could see now the pale blue haze float on the water.

"Once we talked about committing double suicide. It almost happened because all we had to do was to step overboard. It was tempting."

"What made you change your mind?" asked Yuki, thumping his feet in the small boat.

"We were trying to decide when we would do it, but couldn't make up our minds, and kept putting it off. And then we saw two bodies that seemed to have died of double suicide float to the bank across the river. A crowd gathered around them. We also went and stared at them. After we came back to the boat, my lover said, 'Double suicide corpses are not much to look at. We'd better drop the idea.' I thought if I die with this lover, he might be happy for it, but my patron would be sad. I felt sorry for him. Of course, I totally disliked him. Still, I felt part of my heart belonged to this man who couldn't help being so jealous of me."

"We envy you," a young geisha said. "Your stories of those good old days sound so romantic and easygoing. Things are much more frigid and dry nowadays, it's really disgusting."

"I don't think so," said the old geisha, waving her hand. "You have your own good things today. For instance, everything moves faster now than it used to, like electric devices. Not only that, I think today there are more arts and techniques you can use. To me, it's fascinating."

With this subtle encouragement from Kosono, the young geishas again began waiting on Yuki eagerly, making full use of their charms and techniques. The younger one led the game, the elder, subordinating.

Michiko looked very disturbed. In the beginning she was quiet and serene, showing apparent contempt of the group. She separated herself, now and then taking photos of the scenes. Then suddenly she began acting coquettishly toward Yuki, trying to draw his attention from the geishas. Yuki's interest was aroused by the faint scent of this young girl's flesh, a scent that her pitiful aggressiveness barely squeezed out of her immature virgin body. Yuki inhaled deeply. But the excitement was shallow and brief, and it left him quickly.

The young geishas did not seem too happy about Michiko's challenge. But Michiko was Kosono's foster daughter after all. Besides, they were there only because of their profession so they let her have her way. But whenever Michiko's whim shifted somewhere else, the geishas resumed their service. This irritated her all the more. She felt them like flies swarming over her piece of cake. And she dispensed that irritation once or twice on her foster mother.

Nothing seemed to bother the old geisha though. She picked chickweeds on the bank for her canaries or drank beer with cooked taro at the teahouse of the Iris Garden. They were about to have dinner at Yaomatsu Restaurant in the precinct of the Water God Shrine. Michiko stared at Yuki boldly and said, "I'm not going in. I don't want a Japanese dinner. I'm going home by myself."

Surprised, the young geishas offered to accompany her. Kosono laughed.

"No need for that. We'll put her in a taxi." She waved at a taxi. Watching it drive away, she said, "That girl has learned a few smart tricks, hasn't she?"

The old geisha's actions and intentions had become more puzzling for Yuki. He knew now that his first interpretation was mistaken. She was not being good to a young man because she wanted to ease her accumulated sense of guilt. She never hinted that she was interested in him as a young lover, though their imagined relationship was becoming the gossip of the neighborhood. Why was her attitude so permissive toward an adult man she was keeping, Yuki wondered?

Yuki seldom went to his workshop now. He had been neglecting his research, too. The fact that the old geisha said
nothing to him bewildered Yuki all the more about her purpose in helping him. Trying not to look into his workshop
in spite of its glass door, he lay down on the verandah. Now
that summer was coming, thick fresh green leaves were
springing out from old trees in the garden. Azaleas and wall
irises by the rock at the edge of the pond attracted wasps.
The sky was clear and profoundly blue. The clouds that took
shapes of various continents moved slowly, with their color
dulled by impregnated moisture. Paulownia was blooming
in the neighbor garden, half hidden by their clothes drying
on the line.

Yuki missed the days he used to work for Makita. He
went to many strangers' houses. He repaired a connection
in a narrow kitchen closet filled with the smell of moldy soy
sauce, hardly able to move his arms. Often the wife or a
maid of the house where he worked shared part of her lunch
with him. He remembered how much he had detested those
things then, but now he missed them. In Makita's small
upstairs room Yuki used to make estimates for new con-
tracts. Then the children would come up in turns and hug
him sometimes so hard that his neck was swollen red. A
little one took a piece of candy from her mouth and with

her saliva dripping from it like a thread, pushed it into his mouth.

Yuki began to wonder if all he really wanted was to live an ordinary peaceful life. Perhaps he should not attempt as great an enterprise as invention. He thought of Michiko. Though the old geisha kept her aloof profile that showed no knowledge about Michiko and Yuki, in reality she might have planned all along for them to marry so that her old days would be well taken care of. However, this did not seem possible, for as lofty a person as Kosono wouldn't be capable of such a petty exchange.

And Michiko. . . Michiko reminded Yuki of an unripe chestnut, a hard shell, but watery and shapeless inside. He laughed a little. She was a girl whose form was developed more than enough, but whose inner personality was hopelessly empty. It was a bit droll. But there was some change in her attitude recently. She was hostile and antipathetic toward him, yet she somehow seemed to cling tenaciously to him.

Michiko's visits to Yuki's house were not so sporadic these days; it was more regular now, once a day, or every other day.

That day Michiko came in from the back entrance. She opened a screen between the living room and the guest room in which the workshop was installed. She stood upon the rail. Resting one hand on a post and hiding the other in her kimono sleeve, she twisted her body a little as if to pose for a camera.

"I came," Michiko said sulkily giving him a side glance.

"Un huh," was Yuki's only greeting. He was lying down on the verandah. Michiko said the same thing again, and received the same response. She was indignant.

"What a lazy answer. I'll leave and never come and visit you again!"

"You are such a spoiled brat," Yuki sat up and crossed his legs. Then, staring at her, he said, "So, you have a tradi- tional hairdo today."

"So what!" Michiko turned back showing her sulky mood in the back seam of her kimono. The upper half of her body looked attractive enough to Yuki. Her *obi* sash was gorgeous, and her white nape was exposed in the shape of a reversed Mount Fuji right above the large bow of the sash. But from the waist to the bottom hem, her body line was straight as a stem with one flower, exposing the body of a young girl whose sexual charm had not yet bloomed. Yuki was amused with this contrast. He wondered what it would be like if this girl were to become his wife and wait on him, depend on him, and take care of him, telling him this and that. This imagined picture of his future depressed him a little. It seemed so commonplace, so limited. But, one never knows, he thought. And the unknown attracted him. Yuki wanted to find some irresistible charm in her small and almost too finely featured face surrounded by the elaborate hairdo that made her forehead look even smaller.

"Turn around and let me look at you. It's quite becoming."

Michiko shrugged her shoulders and turned to face Yuki. She touched her collar and hair, gesturing to rearrange her appearance.

"Oh, you are such a bother, really. . . are you satisfied?"

Her hair ornament twinkled. Flattered by Yuki's interest in her, Michiko said, "I brought you something good to eat. Guess what it is."

Yuki didn't expect this. How could he allow his thoughts to be read so easily by this little girl!

"I don't want to play a game with you. If you brought something for me, just give it to me."

Michiko rebelled against his high-handedness and turned away from him.

"I was only trying to be nice to you. If you are going to be so pompous, I won't give it to you."

"Give it to me!" Yuki stood up. He walked slowly over to Michiko, his body firm as a person of absolute authority. He was astounded at his own behavior, but he could not help himself.

For the first time in his life Yuki felt severe tension, a tension born of the fear of entrapment into a small petty orderliness and the disgusting helplessness with which he would push himself into that trap. In the struggle not to be defeated by his self-disgust, sweat wet his forehead.

Michiko watched him with contempt, thinking that he was still carrying on his high-handed joke. Then she realized something was different this time, and she became frightened. Still murmuring, "No, I won't give it to you, no, no ..." she backed off to the living room. Yuki, looking fiercely straight into her eyes, drew out his hands from his kimono and pressed them on her shoulders. Michiko was so frightened that she let out a small cry, once, twice. Then suddenly her features began to loosen, stripped of all their pretentious coyness.

"Give it to me, right now!" Yuki was still demanding. The words meant nothing to her. She felt only the thick shivering of Yuki's arms and saw his throat move slowly as he swallowed sour saliva.

"Sorry, I'm sorry." Michiko was half-crying with her eyes wide open. But Yuki, as if electrified, looked pale and idiotic and, fixing his stare on her, kept sending violent shivers through his arms.

Michiko at last understood something about him. She remembered that her foster mother talked often about the timidity of men. Oh, that must be it, Michiko thought. Here is a mature man who is fighting with his own timid shyness over a thing like this. Why, he is like a good-natured cow, something I can pet.

She gained back her control and gathered her features once again into a pretty seductive smile.

"You silly thing. Don't be like this. I was going to give it to you anyway."

She wiped off the cold sweat from Yuki's forehead with her palm. A green breeze swept through the foliage of the garden. She listened to it a second and took his strong arm.

"Come this way, will you?"

It was almost evening. Misty May rain was falling. The geisha came into the garden through a little twig gate, holding an umbrella over her head. She was wearing a muted-colored formal kimono. She came into Yuki's house, let the long train fall on the *tatami* floor and sat down.

"I dropped by on my way to work because there is something I wanted to talk about with you." She took out the tobacco case and drew an ashtray toward her. "I know my daughter comes here quite often. Don't misunderstand me, I have nothing against it. You two are young, so something may happen between you. Well, about that something . . . ." Nothing would make her happier, if they were really in love, she said. "But," she continued, "if it's only a vague feeling you have for each other, if it's just the love of convenience, then it's nothing new. There are a lot of cases like that in life. I myself have gone through that many times. It's the same dull thing, you can go on repeating it."

Whether it is work or love between a man and a woman, the geisha said, she wanted to see a person put his entire soul into it. If she could see that happen, then she would be able to die in peace.

"Don't hurry, and don't be impatient. I want you to strike the right target, whether it is work or love. And if you find it, stick to it."

"I think that's impossible," Yuki laughed. "The kind of purity of soul you talk about doesn't exist in this age. I can't do it."

"In any age you don't find it unless you look for it very hard. You have to try very hard to make it happen. So, take as much time as you need, and if you like, eat lots of *mugitoro* too. But try, try hard to find the right target of your life. You are lucky enough to have this healthy body. Maybe you can go on looking for it for a long time yet," she laughed.

A carriage came and the old geisha went out.

That evening Yuki left the house. For no apparent reason, he decided to go away.

He began to understand what the old geisha wanted from him. She was trying to let him accomplish what she could not have. But that would be impossible. Neither she nor he, nor even the luckiest person on earth, could accomplish what she wanted in this world. The reality in which they lived gave only bits and pieces of the ideal, but never the whole. The ideal whole flickered before their eyes just to tempt them, so that they would keep trying.

He could reason this way, and could accept his limitations, but the old geisha could not. She wouldn't accept her limitations. That was a shortcoming on her part. Yet that shortcoming could also be her strength.

What an old woman she was! Yuki was astounded. She could be turning into a monster after so many years of living! There was something immensely tragic in her aspiration. This impressed him. But at the same time he did not really wish to be trapped in her aspiring and reckless scheme of life. Yuki wanted to get away from the ever-ascending escalator on which she was trying to put him. He would rather cuddle up in a comfortable life as in a down *futon* he made himself. To sort out these many thoughts, Yuki rode on a train for two hours from Tokyo and came to an inn by the sea. The inn was run by Makita's brother and Yuki had been here before to check their electric installment. The sea spread in front. Behind, the mountains stood with the incessant movement of clouds near the peaks. He had never done this before: to come and stay in a quiet place surrounded by beautiful nature, to think by himself, to decide.

He was healthy. He enjoyed eating the fresh fish out of the sea. He enjoyed swimming, too. And he laughed.

He felt a roar of laughter boiling up from inside. It was droll, first of all, that the old geisha, who carried that limitless aspiration within herself, didn't realize it and was living her daily trivial life in the town. It was also droll that Yuki himself could not escape from the geisha's magnet even now, being miles away from her, just as a certain animal cannot go beyond an enclosing line drawn on the ground. It was funny, too, that he chose this inn as the getaway place, thinking that the geisha could locate him easily. It was because, although confined within her reach, he felt oppressed and bored, he knew he would be very lonely without her.

The relationship with Michiko was also funny. Without really knowing what was happening, they touched each other momentarily like a flash of lightning.

After a week in the inn, Makita came with money from the old geisha to take him back. Makita said to Yuki, "I imagine you may have to put up with things you don't like. You'd better find a way to earn your own living and quit depending on her."

Yuki went back with Makita. But after this he often went off alone without warning the geisha.

"Mother, Yuki escaped again, did you know?"

Michiko stood at the entrance to the storehouse in her tennis wear. She seemed to be indulging in the sardonic pleasure of watching her foster mother suffer, while pretending nonchalance. "I don't think he came home last night, or the night before."

The old geisha was sitting in her small orderly studio built in the storehouse of her garden. She was repeating her lessons of new Japanese music after the teacher had left. Hiding the chagrin boiling inside her, she looked up at Michiko with an indifferent expression on her face.

"The man gave in to his bad habit again, didn't he?"

She lit her long pipe and puffed it once, then pulled the tip of her kimono sleeve—today her kimono was of bold striped silk—in a reflex action perhaps to see if it was becoming.

"Never mind, I can't give in to him all the time." And dusting off a few ashes from her knees, she began to fold her music.

Disappointed with the absence of anger in her mother, Michiko left for a nearby tennis court, racket in hand.

But as soon as the daughter had left, the old geisha hurried to the telephone. She called Makita and asked him again to find Yuki. Her voice was shaking as she accused the young

man of his selfishness and lack of responsibility. This was
the young man she was helping. The receiver shook with
her hand. Still, she felt that she was animated by a mellow
loneliness born of fermented fear of losing him.

Away from the telephone, she whispered to herself, "That
young man has a lot of spirit in him. Well, why shouldn't
he?" and wiped her eye with her kimono sleeve.

She respected Yuki a little more each time he ran away,
but she also suffered from a tremendous sense of loss when
she imagined that he might never come back. It would be
an irreplaceable loss.

In midsummer I received several *tankas* from Kosono who
had been taking haiku lessons from my friend. She wanted
me to go over them. It was after dinner and I was enjoying
the cool evening air on the verandah facing the garden with
the pond and the fountain, gifts made by her. A maid handed
me the manuscript. I unfolded it and listened to the sound
of the water, reading the *tankas* with much interest.

I want to introduce here one of her *tankas*, which I think
speaks eloquently for the old geisha's recent feelings. I have
made a slight change in the wording, not from the teacher's
duty but for the purpose of helping the reader understand
the meaning better. The meaning, I assure you, is not al-
tered at all.

Year after year
    Sadness deepens in me,
And my life flourishes
    ever more.

1938

NORTH COUNTRY
(Michinoku)

I**T WAS THE TIME** when Paulownias were in bloom. I was walking close to the Main Street of S-Town in the Northern District. The town was the site of a castle where feudal lords had ruled for hundreds of years.

I was with several prominent members of the community. We had just left a Buddhist Temple where a spacious interior hall had been used for my lecture.

We left the temple gate and were walking along the street by a river well known for its scenic beauty. They wanted to show me the ruins of the castle on the top of the mountain. The whole mountain was enveloped with profuse green foliage, and during the day cuckoos were said to be heard in the woods.

After the lecture, I was still in a state of excitement. My mind was stirred up and I wanted to keep talking, but at the same time, I was glad my lecture was over.

The low, two-storied houses with wide overhangs looked shadowy and uneven along the street. Overhead was the deep blue sky of the north. Through the window one could see a white heap of silkworm cocoons in one of the houses.

"They are collecting spring cocoons," explained one of my hosts. The smell of snowpeas cooking drifted from a nearby house.

There was a barbershop with an old-fashioned signpost of swirling red, blue and white stripes. By the shop was a weeping willow with its voluptuous branches almost touching the earth.

Several houses down from the willow tree, I spotted a dilapidated pseudo-western style house. It was a photo studio. A showcase with a narrow ornamental roof extended from the front wall. I stopped to look in. I was curious, as I always am, traveling through strange places, to see what type of women were considered beautiful and what clothes they wore. I found a picture of a lady, apparently of the upper class, who did her best to imitate Tokyo fashion. There was one of an elderly gentleman who seemed very proud of his beard, a geisha in a curious western costume, the stiff pose of a newlywed couple, two schoolgirls with their hands locked together. I could not help noticing that all these women had large, black, clear eyes. These beautiful eyes must be the distinctive trait of the people of this region.

Glancing through the pictures, my attention was drawn to a rather large photo of a young boy. It was in the center of the showcase and other photos were posted around it. It appeared old and perhaps had been in the case for many years ever since it was taken. Maybe that is why the picture looked a little strange. But there was something else, something strange about the boy himself, particularly about his round, generous face. And that strangeness appealed to my feelings, though I could not explain why.

The boy was wearing an expensive-looking kimono. But his handsomely-featured face had a look of such nonchalance that I wondered how the photographer could capture a natural portrait like this. The camera might not have existed as far as the boy was concerned. My face almost touched the glass of the case as I stared at the picture of the boy.

Seeing what had aroused my interest, one of the people in the group came and stood beside me.

"This is a picture of Shiro-Fool who was rather well known in this area."

Surprised, I repeated his words, "Did you say fool? Was he a fool, an idiot?"

"Yes, he was an idiot, but was no ordinary fool. He was very much liked and well treated by the community."

And they told me the story of this boy, thinking perhaps the story would amuse me.

◆

It must have been before the railways were nationalized, because the train conductors and attendants were said to have given him a free ride whenever he wanted. It must have been about the turn of the century when private railroad companies were more generous and kind to the passengers.

One day, a boy clad in shabby clothes came to town. He stopped in front of a shop, took a broom from the store corner and began sweeping the front street. If the day was dry and dusty, he would also sprinkle water. When finished, he put away the broom and the pail, and stood quietly, facing the shop, with a gentle smile on his face. He looked as though he was waiting for something.

Shopkeepers did not know what he wanted at first. They scolded him and chased him away. The boy went away then, looking very sad. Sometimes a thoughtless servant beat him, and he ran away crying and wailing.

But very soon the boy would forget his bad experiences and begin to smile again. Like a flowing river that could not keep debris on its surface, sadness and sorrow could not stay on his face long. A fresh, bright smile kept reappearing. Soon after he ran away from one shop, he would again be sweeping the storefront of another merchant.

"Could he be begging for food when he finishes sweeping and stands there? That must be it."

People began to understand him.

"It's true, he is begging, but what a gentle, nice way to beg!"

One day a shopkeeper led him to the kitchen, sat him down at the table and served whatever food he could spare at the moment. The boy's face beamed.

Yes, this is what I wanted. Why didn't you understand this before? the boy seemed to be saying as he took *hashi* and began to eat, happy and delighted. There was nothing debasing about his attitude. His manners were both polite and refined. After eating to his heart's content, he said to the shopkeeper very politely, "Thank you very much for the delicious meal."

He always remembered to thank them after he was given meals. If people were too busy with customers, they tried to give him prepared food, rice-balls and such things, wrapped in a piece of paper, rather than taking him to the kitchen and serving him at the table. He would not accept food like that and walked away hungry, appearing almost in pain. This labor was lost, but he began again sweeping for another store. It did not seem to be a real meal for him unless he could sit at a table.

He did not accept money. The few times he did take money, he lost it before he could spend it.

People talked about him.

"He must have been born in a good family."

"That explains his good manners, his politeness."

He said his name was Shiro, but he did not remember his family name. People called him "Shiro-Fool," but some "Dear Shiro-Fool" with an endearing tone in their voices. A rumor began to circulate among the merchants. Once shops are visited by Dear Shiro-Fool, they will do well.

Having explored most of the old castle-town where he first appeared, he took off one day and went to a newly-developed city fifteen miles away. Someone must have taken him on a train.

After this experience, the boy learned to use trains and carriages. He began to wander from town to town and found that he liked traveling. It seemed he could ride on anything free of charge. He went as far north as the tip of Honshu Island and to the southern Japan Sea coast.

He did the same thing in every town he visited; he swept the storefronts and was given meals. Sometimes there were misunderstandings and troubles in the beginning, but soon his innocence and gentleness captured people's hearts.

"The shops Dear Shiro-Fool visits seem to do well." The rumor was superstitious, of course, but at the same time, there was a grain of truth in it. And Shiro's visits became one of necessary experiences shop owners awaited eagerly. The naive, innocent face of the boy, and his unjaundiced behavior, like that of a wandering monk, carried a secret key that triggered one's feelings, shifted the mood of the moment, and brought into one's daily life a lively and vivacious intensity.

People, especially merchants, began to welcome the boy's visit. Some shop owners went so far as to change their clothes to welcome him. Seeing Shiro approach the shop, they put on a formal black kimono and bowed to him. Then they led him into the shop as if to welcome a god of good fortune. Cheerful processions were organized to accompany him to the station. Shiro no longer wore shabby clothes. Merchants now dressed him in silk and satin.

One big town politician with money and power said, "It is good to bring that fool to the town. Business seems to prosper with him around."

F-Town is located at the north end of Japan. In the main street of this town, a kimono merchant had a store. The store building itself was not large, but it had a history of several generations and had a reputation of being well managed. The owner of the store had a young daughter called Ran.

Shiro was very fond of the girl, and whenever he came to F-Town he swept their storefront.

When he finished, he came to see Ran in her living quarters. He seemed to be happy and contented just sitting with Ran. When Ran sewed, he sat there relaxed, occasionally asking simple childlike questions and amusing himself with easy games. When the sun shone into the room he would fall asleep in its caressing warm light. He would wake up once or twice, see Ran still there, feel at ease and go back to sleep again.

Ran took pity on Shiro. In spite of his unpretentious and innocent lifestyle, Ran could see he was afraid of the people around him or what they did. But he trusted Ran completely. With her, he was secure and happy. Ran took care of him, tending his needs, like a sister or a mother.

One day, when they were sitting quietly together, she asked him, "What will you do when I get married and go away?"

Immediately the answer came, "I am coming with you."

Ran laughed, "That's impossible, Shiro. How can I take you with me when I go away to marry?"

Shiro did not understand. "But why can't I come with you?"

"Because when I am married, I will become part of my husband's family and I will have to do what they say. So, unless they say, 'Yes, you can bring Shiro with you,' I can't take you with me. And I doubt that they will say yes."

"Are you saying you will someday belong to somebody else?"

"That's right."

"I see..."

Shiro could understand that. He understood that if Ran married someone else, she would be forever lost to him. He would be left alone, lonely and isolated in this hostile world. He understood it only too well. He could see an enemy towering over him and threatening to snatch Ran away. He became very frightened.

"You cannot marry, Miss Ran, you should never marry!"

"But I have to. Sooner or later every girl gets married."

Shiro was quiet for some time. He was thinking very hard about something. Then he struck his knee with his palm— the gesture was sheer imitation of the adults around him. And he said, "I know what I'll do—I'll marry you myself."

Ran was flabbergasted for a moment, but then she answered, "Well, I think that is a great idea!"

"Yes, sure, I'll marry you." Shiro looked very self-assured.

"If you are really going to marry me, Shiro, I want you to be a wise man, a good man. You know that, don't you?"

Ran said this without much thought, perhaps to encourage him in the difficult life that lay ahead of him.

Shiro never forgot these words of Ran's. Even though his mind was that of an eight-year-old (he was then around sixteen), he must have understood what marriage was.

The summer was maturing even in this northern country. But the heat was not so unbearable in F-Town, nestled in the mountain's breast, because the wind from the south always swept along its streets and carried the heat to the northern sea. Beyond the gentle slope, Mount-Y, which was famous for its folk songs, stood aloof and, at the foot of the mountain, waves of the summer sea glistened now and then through thin mist. There was the smell of sun-dried wheat in the air.

Ran was taking off the basting thread of a new coat she had just finished sewing. She was sitting on the terrace. Occasionally she took her eyes from her work to admire the view of the mountain and the sea. Suddenly she heard loud voices shouting and cheering in the street. They came closer and seemed to stop in front of her father's store. Soon Shiro came into the room. Ran pretended she did not notice him. It was their little game. When he came in, he usually did not say a word and stood there quietly expecting Ran to see him first. It was the only way he knew to demand Ran's attention and perhaps her love. Ran knew this, but she liked to tease him by pretending she did not know he was there.

So Ran kept her eyes downcast for a while and then looked up, as if in surprise.

"But what happened to you, Shiro!" she cried out, genuinely surprised. "Why are you wearing those funny clothes?"

He was wearing a bright red *haori* coat and a big pointed cloth hat in matching red with the point hanging down to the back of his head.

"I said I didn't want to, but they forced me to wear these."

Shiro was almost in tears. Ran was shaking with rage. "Take them off at once!"

With trembling hands Ran helped Shiro take off the ridiculous costume. "They go too far in making fun of you. They cannot do that. It doesn't matter if you are an idiot or not."

Shiro repeated Ran's words, "They go too far in making fun of you. It doesn't matter if you're an idiot or not!"

Shiro always did this. Whatever Ran said, he repeated. Ran's words were words of wisdom for him. Ran used to find this amusing and funny, but today it only made her very sad.

She brought him a cold towel and made him wipe his sweaty face. Then she gave him a chilled bracken starch pastry topped with sugar. Shiro soon got over his fear and quieted down. Sitting close to Ran, he opened up a picture

book for which Ran offered explanation taking her eyes now
and then from her sewing.

"What is this?" Shiro asked pointing to a picture in the
book.

"It's a railway coach."

"What is this, then?"

"A businessman, I guess. You see, he wears western
clothes, and he is carrying a briefcase."

Shiro stared at the figure for a long time, and then said, "I
am going to wear western clothes myself, very soon."

Ran thought he was only imagining things. "Oh really?
That's very nice."

Shiro continued as if he was proud of it. "I'll wear western clothes and I'll sing and dance too."

"What are you talking about, Shiro? Where would you
sing? Why would you wear western clothes? Why would
you do this?"

"I'll sing and dance, and I'll be a wise man, then I'll be
worthy to marry you."

Ran remembered. Yes, she had heard someone mention
that a promoter, using Shiro-Fool's popularity, was trying
to book him into a vaudeville theater. In this case, Ran
thought, this was no joke, this was serious. Ran became
frightened at the image of Shiro performing in a ridiculous
vaudeville show.

"No Shiro, you must not do this. No, don't you see, this is not the way to marry me."

But Shiro was not his usual self. He would not listen to Ran. He would not let her persuade him. "Yes I will, because I must be a really wise and great man to marry you." Shiro stood up and went off. Some greedy promoter must have put it in his mind that the best way for him to marry Ran was to sing and dance in vaudeville.

Soon after that Shiro disappeared from F-Town. A rumor reached Ran that an idiot clad in a costume with gold chains did some entertainment between circus shows and sold trinkets such as old coins and yellow wallet ornaments with a portrait of some kind, which were supposed to bring one good luck.

Ran believed the idiot was Shiro. She was very disturbed and sad. She could not have him doing this. She tried to talk her father into bringing him back to their town. Her mother had died long ago, and Ran did not have anyone else to talk to. But her father, being a practical man of common sense, dismissed Ran by saying, "No use meddling in other people's affairs . . . and anyway, he is an idiot."

Winter came and went; it was spring again. Ran heard that Shiro's popularity had declined and the circus abandoned him. He was now with a small company that put on vulgar shows for country folk. Wearing heavy makeup and being mocked and jeered at by the other players, he performed as a clown in slapstick comedies.

When Ran thought of Shiro in this situation, she felt a great pain as if her whole body was being slashed and tortured. She wanted to save Shiro from the trap he was in, but how to do this, she didn't know. It was only a rumor she had heard about him; she didn't know where he was. If he came back to her, there was no way that she could cure him of his idiocy. Ran prayed to the Shinto gods and to Buddha for Shiro's return.

Many years went by and Ran no longer heard about the boy. Her father died and Ran, being the only daughter, had to take over the store. Before he died he wanted Ran to marry so that she would not be left alone in the house. All the relatives wanted her to marry, and they did their best to persuade her. But Ran refused. Coming from an otherwise obedient and quiet daughter, this stern refusal surprised them.

How it would disappoint him if Shiro should hear that she was married, Ran felt. She wanted to spare him this disappointment. Ran knew this did not make much sense. How could he still expect to marry her?

He might not even remember her. After all, he was only a fool. . . . But this fool somehow touched and captured her heart, though when and how she did not know, but she couldn't help herself. She felt if she had married and lived an ordinary life, Shiro, in some lonely and desolate corner of the world, would have suffered, would have really been crushed. It might be only in her imagination, but her pity for him was real. She would not allow herself to make him suffer, even in her imagination.

One day, when the north sea roared in anger, Ran heard that Shiro was in Hokkaido, the northernmost island, and was driven to doing hard chores for the company. By that time Ran was long past the marriageable age and had given up the idea of finding a husband. She had also resigned herself to the fact that she would never see Shiro again. As far as she was concerned, Shiro was the same as dead.

◆

The story moved me so much that I wanted to know more about these people. So for the few days I stayed there, whenever I saw old women, I asked if they remembered Ran and Shiro. One lady I met at my welcome party told me, "Miss Ran is still alive, I heard. She is still in F-Town. You are giving a lecture in the town, why don't you go and visit her? She will be pleased to see you."

I did not have to look for her. When I arrived at F-Town, Ran was there among the ladies who came to the railway station to meet me. She had grey hair and her body was slightly bent forward. She seemed to have some hearing difficulties, but she carried herself very well, elegant and refined. My expectation of her to be a lonely, tragic figure was completely wrong. She was cheerful and had a wonderful sense of humor, which made her both popular and distinguished among these elderly women.

We drove along the winding road up to the center of the town. Houses were built only on one side of the street; the other side faced the river where frogs made their songs. Ran was one of the three ladies who rode with me in a car. As we drove up the hill, the mountains trailed off on the left, and beyond the foot of Mount-Y we could see the bright white-caps of the sea.

I wanted to ask Ran about Shiro, but hesitated while other people were with us. Then finding her so unpretentious and broadminded, I ventured to mention Shiro's name. She caught the name immediately and said, "Once I gave up on Shiro, thinking he must be dead. But lately I have changed my mind. You see, after all, he is several years younger than I am, and since I am alive, it's possible that he is still alive. If he ever comes back, I will welcome him in my house, make him comfortable and take care of him for the rest of his life. After I made up my mind, I felt so much better, really relieved. I threw away his spirit table. When I thought he was dead I had it made, and have kept it in my family altar. I am now trying my best to locate him. I hope I can find him someday."

I watched her face with fascination. A pale white ray of hope, almost like a shadow, illuminated the face of the old woman who had gone through a rare, strange interplay of human emotions. I thought of the idiot boy whose simple and straightforward passion made so deep an impact on the woman's heart.

I was resting after dinner in a room provided for me by a rich family of the town when I was told that I had a visitor.

It was Ran.

We talked a long while, and when our voices finally trailed off in the silence of the night, I found myself wishing Ran's wishes, and feeling her feelings. I felt I too could wait for Shiro's return. I could be here forever waiting for him...

The lights of the squid fishing boats began to glow on the darkening sea.

1938

THE HOUSE SPIRIT
(Karei)

IN UPTOWN TOKYO high on the hill there is an intersection where two streetcar lines cross. A narrow road goes off from the intersection downhill toward the old town district. Halfway down this hill, across the street from the precinct of Hachiman Temple, stands a restaurant well known for its loach soup.

An entrance to the restaurant is framed by a meticulously polished thousand-bar lattice, and an old *noren*, a short curtain indicating the entrance, hangs down halfway. The letters "LIFE," in traditional style, are dyed white on the curtain.

The restaurant specializes in soups and dishes of loach, catfish, mud-turtle, and swell-fish; and in the summer, bleached whale meat is added to the regular menu. Because these creatures are believed to be a source of rejuvenating energy, the first owner of the restaurant had named it "LIFE."

The name must have been unique at first, but the uniqueness had faded over the years, and people no longer paid much attention to it. Even so, customers had continued to patronize the restaurant because of its special cooking methods and its reasonable prices.

Then, a few years ago, romanticism became the predominant trend of the period and people connected the word "life" with the fascination of tantalizing peril, with adventure born of nihilism, and also with the persistent pursuit of the unknown. After being ignored for a long time, the word on the old, worn curtain at the restaurant entrance had regained a sort of exciting appeal to the young people of the neighborhood. When young students, walking along, happened to see the sign, one of them would say with youthful melancholy, "I'm exhausted, why don't we eat Life?"

Teasingly, another would respond, "Sure, but take care so that you won't be eaten by It." Then they would tap each other's shoulders, and flocking together, enter the restaurant.

The dining area of the shop was one large raised room, its floor covered with a cool rattan *tatami* weaving. On it, rectangular wood boards, supported by short legs, were placed in the shape of a square. These served as tables. Some customers dined there sitting on the rattan, while others sat on the stools that stood on the lower dirt floor. The dishes the customers ordered, mostly soups, were served in small pans or in lacquerware bowls.

The walls were stained by soot, steam, and smoke, but the lower half of the wood panels glowed like red copper because the employees wiped that part often, as far up as they could reach. The upper half and the ceiling were black, which reminded one of the inside of a stove. The room was lighted, even during the day, by a glaring, bare chandelier. The bleaching light gave the place a cave-like atmosphere. It also made the fish bones a customer might take out of his mouth with his chopsticks look like white coral. Under this light, diced green onions, piled on a large platter, glistened like precious stones. The whole scene seemed to resemble a feast of starved demon, partly because the people bending over the dishes gave the impression that they were devouring some forbidden food.

There was an opening, a window, in the center of the dividing wall, and a shelf extended from its bottom. The dishes ready to be served were placed on this shelf from the kitchen and a maid carried them to the tables. Money received from the customers was also put on this shelf. A cashier's counter was set up at the kitchen side of this window. And there, behind a square lattice screen, the pale face of the woman guardian of the shop, the mother, had been seen for many years. She had always sat there, handling money and keeping a watchful eye on the place.

But recently, instead of the mother, the tanned face of her daughter, Kumeko, appeared behind the window. Kumeko would glance through the opening now and then to supervise the maid and survey the activities in the dining area. When her eyes met those of the students, sitting in a group, the students would raise their voices to attract her attention. Then, Kumeko, smiling wryly, would tell the maid, "Bring them a lot of diced garnish onions. That'll quiet them."

Trying to stifle a laugh, the maid would carry to their table a spice box piled high with diced onions. The students, viewing the pile of the fiery vegetable, realized that their challenge had been successful, and they cheered happily.

Kumeko had come back to the restaurant about eight months ago and taken the place of her mother at the cashier's counter. Even since her high school days she had detested this house, which reminded her of a dark cave. She could not accept the family trade which specialized in nourishing the old, weary people who had wasted away their energy.

Why are people so afraid of aging? Why can't they take life as it comes? There is nothing more repulsive, she thought, than a so-called energy source, covered with glistening oil and giving off a penetrating odor. Kumeko was a young woman of delicate nature who could get a headache just by inhaling the scent of fresh summer oak leaves. She preferred the evening moon, seen through thin foliage, to fresh oak leaves, perhaps because she herself was satiated with her own youth.

For many generations, it had been the family tradition for the men to take care of the buying and the cooking, and for either the wife or the daughter to look after the cashier's counter. And because Kumeko was the only daughter of the family, she would have no choice but to marry a man, any man, and become the woman guardian of this starved demon's cave.

The mother, after lifelong endurance of her family duty, seemed to have lost her personality. Her face now showed nothing but white and gray shadows, like a Noh mask. A chill ran down Kumeko's spine when she thought that some-day she, too, would be like her mother.

When she finished high school, Kumeko left her parents' home and found herself a job. She never said anything about her life during the three years she had stayed away from home. The only contact she made was to send occasional postcards to her family. Of these three years, even Kumeko herself remembered little except that she had fluttered about her lively work places like a butterfly, touching male friends with her antennae, as ants might greet each other. The entire period could have been a dream, and it had been very boring because she merely repeated the same activity again and again.

When Kumeko's mother was taken ill, one of their relatives had contacted her and told her to come home. People did not see any change in Kumeko, except perhaps that she had grown a little.

The mother asked her, "What have you been doing all this time?"

Kumeko merely laughed off the question. There was an echo in her laugh, like a fresh breeze, that seemed to ward off any further prying. And her mother was by no means an inquisitive person. She simply said, "I must ask you now to take over the cashier's counter."

Kumeko again laughed a little by way of consent. The family never had had serious talks among themselves; such talks seemed to embarrass them. Kumeko resigned herself to accepting her fate, and showing little resentment, began to work at the cashier's desk.

It was close to New Year's Eve. The wind was blowing sand off the downhill road and the wooden sandals of passers-by clacked on the frozen ground. The sound made the very roots of one's hair shiver on this cold night. The wind carried the squeaking noise of the streetcars at the intersection into one's ears, and the rustle of the foliage near the Hachiman Temple mingled with the squeak. It sounded like a blind man's murmur from far away.

If I went out and looked down at the city from the top of the hill, Kumeko thought, the lights below might be flickering like fishing fires on the winter sea.

After the last customer had left, the room was filled with the smell of boiled-down food and with cigarette smoke, which dimmed the light from the chandelier. The maid and a delivery man had collected leftover charcoal from small hibachi stoves in the stone fireplace and were warming themselves.

The night depressed Kumeko. Trying to break her mood, she leafed through a number of fashion and movie magazines. There was still more than an hour until ten, when the restaurant closed.

There won't be any more customers coming in tonight. I might as well close the shop, Kumeko was thinking when the other deliverer, a young boy, came in, shivering from the cold night.

"Tokunaga ordered again, Miss. I was passing in front of his house when he caught me and asked me to deliver an order of loach soup and rice. What shall I do?" he asked.

The maid, who was bored and waiting for something to happen, looked up and said, "He has some nerve! He already owes more than one hundred yen. How dare he order anything before paying something back?"

The maid glanced at the window to see how the cashier would respond.

"It's a problem, isn't it?" Kumeko said. "But since my mother used to allow him as much credit as he wanted, I don't see what we can do except fill his order again."

The older delivery man, who had been warming himself quietly at the fireplace, looked up and, rather unexpectedly said, "No, no, Miss. I don't think you should do it this time. You see, this is the end of the year, our balance settling time. I think you'd better see that his account is cleared. Otherwise, it'll be the same story all over again next year."

This delivery man was acting as supervisor of the employees and his words carried some weight. So Kumeko agreed.

"Ok, then, we won't make the delivery tonight."

Hot curry noodles, topped with fried bean curd, were served to the workers from the kitchen. Kumeko, too, received a steaming bowl. A fire watchman on his round usually arrived after they had finished this night snack. When the sound of his wooden clappers sent sharp vibrations into

the thin glass of the front door it was time to close the shop,
even if it was not quite yet ten.

Just then, the shuffling noise of straw slippers approached,
and they saw the front door open very quietly. The bearded
face of old Tokunaga appeared.

"Good evening. Oh, it's really cold tonight, isn't it?"

The people in the shop ignored him. The old man paused
a while, trying to gauge their reaction, then, tilting his head,
he said in a small, cunning voice, "I wonder. . . well. . . isn't
my order of loach soup and rice ready yet?"

The delivery boy who had taken the order began his lame
excuses.

"I am sorry about that, but when I got back here, it was
already after closing time. So, they couldn't . . . ."

The older delivery man stopped him with a stern glance
and, his chin pointing at him, told the boy, "You can tell
him the truth."

The boy now went on to explain that the old man's debts,
though each order cost only a moderate amount, already
exceeded one hundred yen and it would upset the year-end
account balance of the restaurant unless he paid at least
something, even a small amount.

"And, as you can see, the young mistress, not the madam,
is now in charge of the cashier's counter."

The old man rubbed his hands nervously.

"Oh, I see," tilting his head again, "but it's awfully cold out there. May I come in, anyway?" he asked.

Rattling the door he came into the shop. The maid did not offer him a cushion, so he sat on the bare, cold rattan floor. Sitting alone at the center of the large room, he looked like a criminal who was awaiting his sentence. Though he appeared plump, it was mostly the layers of clothes he was wearing. He seemed well-built, but he did not seem to be in good health. His left hand, slipped through the front fold of his kimono, clutched the ribs on his right side. It was a habit. His gray hair was smoothly combed back. His features were finely chiseled; they seemed to suggest he was enduring a tragic destiny. His fine face reminded one of a Confucian scholar, but his clothes were shabby and threadbare. His *obi* sash was narrow and wrinkled, and he had a long, rectangular apron tied in front. Brown drawers showed below the hem of his kimono, contrasting with a pair of black corduroy *tabi* socks.

The old man began to talk seriously, engaging the daughter in the cashier's window and the employees as his audience. He talked about the economic depression, and the lack of demand for his work, which was artistic metal carving. It was a roundabout way of making excuses for his inability to pay his debts. Then as though to give greater weight to his excuse, his talk went into the rarity of the kind of work he did.

While he spoke, his manner suddenly changed. He assumed an enthusiastic, almost haughty air.

"My kind of carving is called *katakiri-cho*, or halfway-cut carving. It's different from ordinary carving. It is a technique of cutting metal with metal, and it's extremely difficult to master. It demands tremendous strength and willpower. To do this kind of work, to keep myself going, I need rich food like your loach soup everyday."

Like many old master craftsmen, Tokunaga often would forget the purpose of his talk, losing himself in the talk itself. He put on a one-man show, totally self-absorbed, using plenty of gestures, explaining proudly about his work. It was an ancient art form, he said, but was restored about three hundred years ago to its present height by Somin Yokoya, who was the great master of the Genroku Period. If one sought an analogy in samurai sword fighting, this art would be like a one-blow match.

He paused then, holding an imaginary burin in one hand and a hammer in the other. Firmly stabilizing his body, inhaling deeply through the nose, he gathered all his strength at his abdomen. His form was perfect, though he was presenting only a gesture, an imitation. It was flexible, yet immobile and resistant to all outside forces. It was a stance firmly built upon the laws of nature. The delivery man and the maid, who had been huddling near the fireplace, came away from it and sat up straight. The awesome tension in the old man's performance must have affected them.

The old man relaxed then, and let out a short laugh.

"You see, if it's an ordinary type of metal carving, you can do it in this way, or that way, using only your hands."

Like a comedian, he was very good at showing collapsed forms in exaggeration. Bending his back, he handled the imaginary tools with only the twist of his wrists. The delivery men and the maid giggled.

"But with my kind of carving, it's different."

The old man resumed his former grand stance, closing his eyes in meditation. As he slowly opened his eyes, which were shaped like lotus petals, he cast a slanting dark glance down upon the imagined tool in his left hand. Holding that hand in a fixed position, he stretched his right arm straight from the shoulder, and threw it down in a beautiful arc toward the fixed hand.

Kumeko had been watching this performance through the cashier's window. The gesture reminded her of the beautiful, firm arm of a plaster model of a famous Greek sculpture she had seen. It was a young discus thrower, she remembered, and the arm was stretched to its utmost limitation. In the tension and vigor of the old man's striking motion, Kumeko sensed a desperate joy of creation, combined with a hatred of destruction. There was something superhuman about the speed of his motion.

His hammer hand, moved in an arc that could be the infinite motion of stars following their orbits, suddenly stopped with absolute determination, just before striking the burin hand. In repeating the motion it stopped always at the exact same distance from it. There could have been an impenetrable disc right there in the air. Would one call this artistic discipline?

The old man relaxed again.

"Did everyone see it?" he asked. "I hope you understand. You see, I cannot go on with my work unless I have your loach soup."

Actually, this was not the first time the old man had put on a show. Rather, it had been his routine. But whenever the show was given, the people around him would forget that they were in a restaurant in Tokyo and became totally immersed in a dangerous pleasure and a wild, yet disciplined freedom created by his performance.

The people in the restaurant gazed at his face with renewed interest. Then they burst into laughter when his performance, as usual, ended with a plea for loach soup. The old man was embarrassed, but hiding it, he began again.

"There are two ways of using the blade of the burin, that is to say, yin and yang."

Again he took the proud stance of a master craftsman. His talk now was about the artistry of handling the blade. By applying either one of these two methods, he explained, one could carve the efflorescent life of a peony, or the grand and virile life of a Chinese lion. With more accentuated gestures he spoke of the profound challenge to recreate living things upon a hard, flat metal plate; and this only through his skill. His eyes had become dreamy, as if in an ecstasy of drinking sweet drops of nectar.

That, however, began to bore his audience because they could see the old man was now indulging himself in a private pleasure permitted only to the performing artist.

So, to stop him, someone said, "Well, in that case, maybe we can deliver your order one more time. Why don't you go home and wait for it."

The old man got up and went out. They closed the shutter of the entrance behind him.

That night too, the wind was blowing hard. A night watchman had gone by sounding his wooden clappers. The heavy shutter of the front entrance of the shop had been closed and the employees had gone to a nearby bathhouse. As if watching them leave the old man had come in stealthily through the side door.

He now sat facing the opening behind which Kumeko was still working. He sat there alone for a while, looking uneasy and awkward. It was close to midnight. He had an air of determination, and yet he seemed very gentle.

"Ever since I was a young man," he began, "I have had a taste for this little fish called loach. The kind of work I do really cuts me to the bone marrow, you know. And I just have to eat something that can keep me going. For twenty years now, after I failed in life and came to live in this poor neighborhood, in my loneliness and misery, this little fish, which looks like a willow leaf with fins attached, has become something more to me than just food."

As though murmuring a lover's complaint, the old man began to relate his story in little sequences.

Even when he was fiercely angry like a demon in hell for being slandered and envied by others, he said, if he put the little fish in his mouth, and chewed its head and bones with his front teeth, his rancor would go away and gentle tears would fill his eyes.

"I feel pity for the fish for being eaten, but I pity myself too for eating it. Everybody is pitiful, yes, that's all. I didn't want a wife, but there were times when I longed for something dear and sweet. If that longing began to get out of hand, I ate the little fish and it always calmed me down."

He brought a terry-cloth handkerchief out of the chestfold of his kimono and wiped his nose with it.

"I don't mean to embarrass you," he went on, "but your mother was a kind and understanding person. Once before, when I had no money to pay my debts, I came in here to make excuses. It was late at night, too. She was sitting there by the window, just as you are now, wearily resting her cheek on her hand. She looked out of the opening and said to me, 'Mr. Tokunaga, if you want our loach soup, you can have as much as you like, and any time you want it. Don't worry about your debts. I would like to ask you one thing, though. When you make a hair ornament which you think is your masterpiece, you can give it to me as your payment, or I can buy it from you. That's all I ask, that's all I ever want from you.' She said this many times to me."

The old man wiped his nose again, then he went on.

"Your mother was young then, about your age maybe, because she married young. I felt sorry for her because her husband was a playboy, having fun in the red lantern districts of Yotsuya and Akasaka. Your mother had to put up with it, and she had to stay at this window. She never moved away. Though she sat here quietly, sometimes I could feel that she desperately needed someone to relate to, to rely on, to cling to. Of course, it's only natural, she was a living woman, not a dead stone."

Tokunaga, too, had been young then. He could not bear to witness the young wife wasting away. More than once, he had thought seriously about tearing her away from this window, even by force. But, at the same time, he had wanted to get away from her. What would become of me, he thought, if I should be caught by this mummy-like woman? When he gazed at her face, he lost the courage to act. Her face seemed to be saying to him, "If I ever made a mistake with you, an irrevocable curse would forever be set upon me by this house. It would be a curse impossible to erase, no matter how hard I tried. But, if there were no one in the world to offer me some compassion, some warmth, I would soon collapse like ashes."

"With my art I thought I could offer at least breath of life to your mother. I could offer a little rejuvenating energy to this woman who was slowly being fossilized alive. I put my whole being into my hammer and burin. And the kind of halfway-cut carving I do was the ideal means to absorb my devotion."

Striving hard to produce something that might please her mother, he had mastered a carving skill comparable only to Natsuo Kanoh, who was the great master of the Meiji Period. But there were few masterpieces through which his life might shine. Tokunaga gave the mother the best hair ornament out of a hundred, and sold several better ones to earn his living. The rest, finished and unfinished works together, he threw into a recasting furnace, for they did not satisfy him.

"Your mother adorned herself with the hair ornament I made for her, and from time to time she took it off and looked at it in her hand. She looked very young and alive when she did that."

However, Tokunaga had been doomed to remain obscure. That could not be helped.

"But the passage of time is a cruel thing, " he said. "First I carved a weeping cherry on the flat surface of a large silver ornament, with two long pins attached to it. That was meant for a young woman's hairdo. The next thing I created was a smaller, ball-shaped one. On the ball I carved a summer chrysanthemum and a cuckoo. Then I did a delicate hairline carving of red and bush clover, on a tiny piece shaped like an earpick. By that time my art wasn't of much use. The kind of ornaments used by middle-aged women didn't have enough space for carving. It was several years ago that I made my last one for your mother, a classical, one-pin hair jewel. And on its neck I carved only a sandpiper, calling its mate. Really, there wasn't much I could do."

Suddenly Tokunaga looked totally exhausted. "To tell you the truth, I have no hope of paying you back. My health is declining and I have lost passion for my work. Your mother won't live long now and she doesn't need my hair ornaments anymore."

"Only I feel I cannot live through this cold night unless I have some loach soup and a bowl of rice. Without them my body will be cold and numb. With us metal carvers each stroke might be the last one. We don't think of tomorrow. If you are the daughter of that mother, could you please let me have a few of these little fish. Even if I am to die soon, I don't want it to happen on such a cold winter night. At least for one more night, tonight, I want to live by chewing and eating the life of the little fish, sucking their life into my bones."

In his plea he looked like an Arab praying to the setting sun. With his face slightly upturned, yet crouching like the guardian dog of a shrine, he repeated his pathetic supplication like a magical chant.

Hardly aware of what she was doing, Kumeko got up from her cashier's window. Almost in a trance, she walked unsteadily toward the kitchen. The cooks were all gone, the kitchen deserted. Only the sound of water dripping into the tank of the live fish filled the room.

One ceiling light had been left on, and Kumeko could see a large covered jar. She took off the lid and there were loaches in it, soaking in *sake* in preparation for the next day. Some were still alive and eerily thrust their heads up above the surface. The small fish which she had detested all her life now seemed very dear to her. She rolled up her sleeves and put her bare, tanned arm into the jar and caught a loach. She put it in a small pan. She caught another, then another. The small fish wriggled in her clutching fingers. The vibrations, like electric waves, reached her heart. At that instance, she felt she heard a soft, mysterious whisper, a response of life.

Kumeko poured stock and soy sauce into the pan, added shredded burdock, and brought the mixture to a boil on top of the gas stove. She turned off the gas and poured the hot soup into a large red lacquered bowl. The little fish floated in the soup with their white undersides up. She placed a pinch of chopped Japanese pepper leaves in the indented hold of the lid of the bowl, and she slid it through the window, together with a tub of cooked rice.

"I'm afraid the rice may not be warm enough."

Exuberant with joy, the old man immediately was on his feet, kicking up the soles of his corduroy *tabi* socks. He took the fish bowl and the rice, carefully put them into one of the shop's delivery boxes, opened a side door and, like a thief, quietly stole out into the dark.

The mother, who had been bedridden for some time, became more cheerful after she had found out that she had terminal cancer. She said that at last her declining health allowed her to do as she pleased. She had her *futon* bedding brought into a warm room lit by the early spring sun. Sitting up there and eating whatever food she felt like, she talked to Kumeko in an intimate tone she had never before used with her daughter.

"It's very strange, you know, for many generations the women of this family who ran the business had prodigal husbands. My mother had one, so did my grandmother. Oh, it's really a shame! But, if you put up with it and patiently stay at the cashier's window, our restaurant somehow keeps going. And the strange thing is that somebody always comes around to give you his sincere devotion. My mother had a man like that, my grandmother too had one. So, I am telling you now, if fate should be cruel to you in the future, you must not be discouraged."

Just before she died, the mother put on thin makeup, saying that her face looked disagreeable, and asked that a box once used for *koto* bridges be brought to her from the closet.

"This is the only real gift to me." She held the box to her cheek and shook it a few times, very affectionately. Inside the box tinkled the gold and silver hair ornaments Tokunaga had made with love and devotion. Listening to the sound, her mother let out a little laugh. It was almost the laugh of an innocent young girl.

Since her mother's death, Kumeko's days are filled with tangled thoughts and feelings. There is an uneasy but strong courage that helps her to face her fate bravely. There is also a lonely yet fervent belief that she could be happy. When her thoughts become too confused, she puts them aside. Petting their entangled mass, as one might stroke a dog, with the fingertips of her emotion, she vaguely thinks about her youth.

Sometimes, she walks to the top of the hill with a group of students, whistling the National Flag March with them. Beyond the valley, above the city, the mist hangs low from the sky.

Kumeko stands there for a while, sucking a piece of candy a student has offered her, and she toys with an amusing fantasy: Who among these young men might become her future prodigal husband, and who might be her eager savior?

But soon she will say, "The shop must be busy," and, embracing her own breasts with her kimono sleeves, she walks back alone to sit behind the cashier's window.

Old Tokunaga comes every night to beg for loach soup, growing more gaunt, and slowly withering.

1939

THE RIVER
(Kawa)

A RIVER FLOWS by her ear. The white caps of ripples remind her of the white teeth that have yet known no lies. The river flows by her ear....

Stars fall upon the ripples some nights, as if white petals of plum flowers were scattered over them. Other nights, the moon falls upon them, and sadly breaks into pieces on the surface. Soon they will be swirled into the restless water. Occasionally, pebbles at the bottom can be seen vaguely through the moon-lit water. The pale blue pebbles seem to be absorbed deeply in their thought, quiet and motionless.

The river in the morning has a color of loneliness, a color that has just awakened from the deep sleep of night. In winter, a bitter wind strikes the river, and the ripples seem to weep like a young girl. Sometimes, one can hear an oriole flapping its wings; the flapping slows down as if to listen to the pleasing sounds of the rippling water.

Suddenly, the silence of the river is broken by the blast from a gun. Somebody must be shooting nearby. The woods along the river are said to be full of birds.

The stream sounds rather sleepy, tired and coarse during the day. The water is clear but there is a hint of grey in it. Yet, one can see duckweeds floating. The water looks warm; if one could feel it, perhaps it is really warm. The color of the water changes in the evening, especially when it showers. Then, little rapid waves make that lonely sound, the same sound created by the mist rustling through thick bamboo leaves. But the river flows on, unchanged, murmuring, unjaundiced, unhurried, never stopping, never stagnant, always flowing, flowing with the innocent stream of her life, always flowing by her ear.

It is her love and incessant longing for the river and its memories that have created, all these years, a phantom stream that never stops running by her ear. No matter where she goes, the river is there, flowing with her.

She was born and grew up by a river. She did not know, not having much interest in the geography of the area, where the river originated. It could be the Kai or Chichibu mountains. Wherever it was, there must be, she imagined, abundant crystals in the area, and from those clear or purple crystals, the first drops of the river water seep down day and night. Cherry petals must scatter upon the crystal mountains in spring.

The river was full in spring. The water in deep quiet pools was often tinted pale pink by cherry blossoms hanging above them, but when it ran through rapids the water burst into white stormy splashes.

When a raft came along with a raftsman tactfully pushing a long green bamboo pole, the white spray of water fell like powdered snow. As the raft floated along, it created a long white train, a galloping white horse spouting white foam from its mouth. But the bow of the raft slid smoothly, undisturbed by the white turmoil it created in its wake. It was so smooth that the bow and the water became one. The raftsman seemed to possess a magical power and, with his quick barefoot steps, appeared to run upon the water. He was singing, too. The song with its melancholy tune of the mountain region was both suited and unsuited to the quick motions of his body. Even so, with his song peacefully resounding over the river, the raft floated on . . . .

It was early summer evening when she went alone to the bank of the river. She threw herself on the grass wishing that the river god would emerge from the water and take her, take her virgin body in his arms and thrust it open with his blazing sword. White, wild roses were in bloom, clustered about her bed of grass. The white flowers shone like pearls in the twilight, making a bed of pearls sprinkled with aromatic dew. The bed seemed to welcome her virgin body.

It was happening to her now. She was beginning to feel desire. And it was perhaps her awareness of the desire that was causing her physical as well as emotional problems. She longed for, but at the same time rebelled against, all that was clinging, shadowy, heaped and swaying. These things troubled her and she could not eat meat or fish or anything that somehow suggested these qualities.

As a daughter of a traditional, prominent family, she knew she should not have left home at this hour of the day, but she dared to break the rule and come to the river bank. She lay there veiled in the twilight mist on the pure, cold bed of wild roses. The thorns of the roses pricked her body through the thin summer clothes she wore. Her body felt the pain, but the pain was mild and even friendly. She welcomed it, it seemed to soothe her burning sensation.

She lay on her stomach. The smell of the wild roses tickled her nose, too strong at first, but soon she adjusted to it. Five minutes. . . ten minutes, yes, now she was quite used to it. Her burning desire was calmed. It was replaced by a merry sort of nonchalance. She placed a thin magazine she brought with her on the grass and, resting her elbows upon it, put her chin between her palms which opened like a sea shell. She watched the river silently. The white caps of the waves were chewing the dark into little pieces. They could be the white teeth of the river god, she thought. She welcomed them, it was such a soothing vision.

The virgin wanted the river god to tear her body, to take her. If anyone were to take her, he would have to be a god, not a human. The desire of man and woman and their enjoyment of sex seemed shameful to her. She felt it was not only shameful, but oppressive and somehow dirty. Two couples and ten children lived in the big house she had just left to come to the river. The thought that she was one of those people bothered her. She felt ashamed of it, and a shadow of this shame crept into her thoughts and bowed her head, even when she was alone.

It was strange. . . when she became aware of the desire, the sexual desire of the people around her became repugnant to her virgin self. She did not want to meet a man and be possessed by him. She would much rather have the river god possess her. She would welcome his white blade that could thrust her mercilessly and purge this helpless, irritating thirst of her body.

"Where are you? Please answer me." She heard a man's voice. It was Naosuke's. His meticulous steps were approaching on the grassy bank. "Where are you? Answer me, please!"

Once more, if he calls me once more, then I shall answer him, she thought. He must have been sent out by my mother to look for me.

"Please, where are you?" She detected concern in his voice, which conveyed something more than just a dutiful search.

Yes, she knew. She had become aware recently that Naosuke was in love with her in his own secret way. But she chose to ignore it. She did not want to think about it. She felt it was enough for her to like him as someone she could trust and rely upon, someone who was always near her whenever she needed him. She wanted to ignore it because love or passion in human terms was repugnant to her. She was going through a difficult period of adolescent changes. For her unstable state of mind, human emotions were too heavy, too ripe, perhaps.

Naosuke came to work for her father as a young apprentice. She was eleven then. It had been six years now. Naosuke had just finished elementary school in a little mountain village about ten miles away from her house. He was the son of a farmer, but came to work for her father, who was a big landowner in the region, to learn land management.

He was a beautiful young boy, always wearing cotton clothes of solid blue, which his mother dyed, wove and sewed for him. He never wore *kasuri*, the white dotted blue which was the usual costume of young apprentices, or the striped cotton welcomed by dandy young men of the manager class. Naosuke's was a simple kimono with narrow straight sleeves, but on him it was extremely becoming.

She knew that Naosuke was in love with her. But she never said anything about it to him. Every morning he walked with her to the bridge she had to cross on her way to school in the city. In the evenings again he met her there to accompany her home. The road from the bridge to her house was desolate and lonely, and her parents did not wish her to walk alone.

Naosuke grew up to be a very quiet young man. No tune was ever heard on his lips, nor did he follow the fashion of other young people by going to a Christian church on Sundays, which many young men believed offered a smart lifestyle garnished with new knowledge. Instead, he was reading the poems of Saigyo, the priest-poet of the middle ages, and *Hakkenden*, the fantastic story of the eight dogs that took human forms and led extraordinarily adventurous lives. He seemed to be quite taken by Hans Christian Andersen's *The Story of the Moon* which her brother lent to him. He never went out with young men of the neighborhood after dark. When the farm workers in her household were busy, he went out in the field and worked all day with them. His skin had never tanned or acquired a coarse farmer look. And yet, he was not a pale, sickly-looking young man, either. He was—well, how could you describe it—one of those people who have very black hair and, as if the black called for an extreme opposite, remarkably fair skin. This

smooth, fair skin gave Naosuke a healthy complexion that
made him very attractive. His limbs were sturdy and flexible, the result of many years of outdoor labor. His body
emitted the fresh scent of the mountains, meadows, field
and trees.

"I am reading Greek mythology," she told him one day.
"See, right here, it is about the river god. It goes like this:
'The ancient Greeks believed that the god of the river can
take any form he chooses. He lives either in a cave at the
bottom or near the source of the river. His disguised forms
vary according to the width, length and forms of the river.
He can be a little boy, a young man or an old man. When
the river flows winding on the flat plain, he can be a snake;
if it is in the rapids, he can become an ox. . . ' Well, there is
much more about him in this book."

Naosuke, who was listening attentively, suddenly spoke
out "It's just what I thought of the river as a child."

"Oh, really? What did you think of it? Tell me."

"I always thought the river was alive. The upper stream
of this river by which I lived is much narrower, and the
surface seems more tense, alive. My mother was a gentle
woman and her feelings were very easily hurt. So, even when
I was in trouble I didn't want to tell her. When I was feeling
sorry for myself after losing a fight with neighborhood boys,

or being unable to afford what I wanted, whenever I felt sad and lonely, I shut myself in my little room and watched the river through a hole in the *shoji* screen. I thought the river understood me, it understood human feelings. Seeing me like this, watching the river for many years, my mother thought I was watching rafts on the river, and she told me that if I was so fascinated by them, maybe I could become a raftsman myself."

"That would have been nice, I think they are wonderful—their muscles, their skills, you know. . . . Why didn't you become one?"

"But I didn't want to. You see, the raftsmen are always going down the river, the sea is their inevitable destination. I didn't like that. I didn't want to go to the sea."

"Don't you like the sea?"

"No, not really, it's too fulsome, too excessive, too rich for my taste."

Yes, that may be, she thought, the sea is too rich and heavy for a youth like him, there is too much life in it. She was surprised that the river god of the Greek myth should trigger Naosuke's interest and make him exceptionally talkative. She wondered if the mysterious power of the river even today had a spell on him.

"How does the river seem to you now?" she asked.

"Well, it's hard to say. . . you know, somehow in my mind, the river and YOU have become one, mingling together. So you see, it's hard for me to say just how I feel about the river. But, how about you? How does the river seem to you?"

"Well, it seems to me like an elderly gentleman with a wonderful stature, refined and accomplished. Do you want to read more about the river god? If you do, you can borrow this book." She handed the book to him.

She was losing her appetite. She could not eat rich food. Rich food with an animal smell, and ripe fruits made her sick. They somehow reminded her of the sexual energy of middle-aged men and women. The only foods she could tolerate were some unripe fruits, salted rice crackers, dried seaweed and candy that did not contain milk. So, there was not much she could eat.

When there was no one watching her, she peeled off the bark of a small willow branch, and bit into the white core. It tasted, she thought, like the unspoiled, pure skin of nature itself. As her teeth squeezed out the pale green sap, it seemed to revive her, restore her strength for an instant.

Because of poor nutrition, her eyesight was weakening, and the river appeared to her all the more vague and mysterious. It might be the scarves of heavenly maids undulating, or thousands of gossamer threads, all gathered and floating down the stream, presenting the mysterious landscape of water and reeds. The countless threads on the surface soon disappeared, then came back momentarily, glistening, undulating, but only to disappear again. She thought she saw a scarf, a part of the garment the river god wore, but the god himself was never seen by her. She sought him, looked into the river very hard, but still could not find him. She became impatient with herself; why can I not find him? Her eyes were strained and tired, and she had to close them. With her eyes closed she had a vision, a vision highly charged with emotional beauty that made her heart pound.

I am worried about our oldest daughter, " her father remarked to his wife, "her health seems to be failing these days."

"Yes, I am aware of it myself, but she is a healthy child basically. She has a good body, so, if only she ate normally she would be all right."

"Maybe Naosuke can go out and buy some plain-tasting river fish that does not offend her," her father suggested.

Naosuke was called in and told by her parents what to do. He said he would be very happy to do anything to help gain her health back. Naosuke was in the corridor, on his knees, when he was told this. She was sitting behind her parents, and she caught a glance of his face. He seemed to be grinning, an ominous grin that sent a chill down her spine. She felt her whole body shaking. Was it possible that even Naosuke nurtured a devilish thought in his mind? The grin he unconsciously showed was almost that of a savage who was about to capture a young woman. A savage might have shouted and cheered at the top of his voice, but Naosuke only grinned silently. Did he intend to cast a spell over the fish he would bring home? Was it his wish to capture her heart with the help of the mysterious river power?

"No, no, father, I don't want Naosuke to do that," she protested.

But before her father could say anything to her, Naosuke was speaking. "Yes, of course I would very much like to do this for your daughter. I will find her a small fish, absolutely fresh that has very little smell. I know what to look for."

From that day on, Naosuke, basket in hand, was seen along the river. "Do you have a small fresh fish to sell?"

Coming back from one of his expeditions, Naosuke would tell her parents, "Cherries are in full bloom now in the upper stream region." On another day, he said, "I went downstream today. There, the green foliage is already very thick."

He showed what he had bought that day to her parents, and went into the kitchen to prepare the fish for dinner himself. He made skewers from a freshly cut bamboo, and barbecued the fish on charcoal. When it was done, Naosuke followed the maid who brought the dish to the daughter. Kneeling by her, he said, "It's ready. Please eat some."

Why is he so eager to make me eat it? True, he was told to take care of my food by my parents. It was an order. Even so. . . . She remembered that ominous grin on his face, and the strange light that came into his eyes when he was told this by her father. Then she remembered the chill she felt. No, she did not want to fall into his trap, if this was his trap. She had to be careful. No, she must not eat fish.

"No Naosuke, I don't want to eat them. They all have such a fishy smell, I hate them."

"But at least you can look at them. Could you do that much?" There was an entreating tone in Naosuke's stammering voice.

All the river fish Naosuke brought her were the size of her little finger. They looked very endearing to her. The deep blue color of the back of the fish faded away toward the belly, and the tiny scales looked as if they were carved on the body with the point of a needle. There was a shade of pink on the belly. Perhaps it was an innate maternal instinct, drawing her to tiny things such as the palm of a baby, that helped her overcome her adolescent whimsicality, her fastidiousness. She ate one little fish. The taste was so plain and gentle, it did not even suggest any sort of flesh. She could eat it now. A minute piece of duckweed secretly placed in each of the tiny fish gave them a subtle flavor. The smell of burnt soy sauce evoked a rustic but pleasing atmosphere.

The bamboo skewer that held several fish together produced its own smell, adding another delicate shade of taste.

"Where did you learn to fix a dish like this? Usually men don't know how to cook, do they?"

"We, who grow up by the river, learn many things from the river. It teaches us what we need to learn," Naosuke answered like a real country boy.

Though she liked the fish, she felt she must not yield to her appetite, must not yield to Naosuke. No, not yet. And she said, "I don't particularly like these fish. But you are very nice to go to so much trouble to bring them to me. So I will do something for you in turn." She hated to be indebted to anyone. If she was, she felt her spiritual independence was threatened. "I would like to give your mother a roll of fabric for her kimono. Will you take it to her?"

Naosuke thought for a while with his head down, and then said, "I don't understand why you are giving something. But if it is for my mother, I'll be very happy to accept it."

She watched Naosuke's back as he carried away the plate on which most of the blue fish were left uneaten. She felt sorry for him, wanted to say some kind words to him, but couldn't. The blue color of his thin cotton kimono was faded around his shoulders. The sun had bleached it during his long walks searching for young, small fish for her.

It was the season when young sweetfish were coming back against the flow of the stream. Azaleas bloomed on the bank and the bushes had young leaves that looked like flowers. Among the dark evergreen foliage, tall spring branches of hemlock trees shot out, and when the wind blew through the branches they undulated like saffron-colored hair. The wheat covering most of the field was now sending shoots like green flames up into the air.

Recently, a young artist from the big city had been coming to visit her family. One day he said to her, "I am not too fond of Van Gogh when he seems intoxicated by the sun, but, standing in this beautiful May field, I feel such an affinity with him and find myself passionately in love with the artist." He was a handsome young man with a rather ornamental quality that reminded one of certain rococo figurines. He was wearing a soft velvet smock and a red velvet tie which suited him extremely well.

Her mother was the first one to be taken in by him. "If that bright refreshing young man could come more often and spend more time with our daughter, she might be able to grow out of those whims and strange eating habits that are making her so ill. . . ."

Her father and brother both agreed. The manners of the young artist were so refined and formal that none of them thought a chaperon was needed for her.

Naosuke took an immediate liking to the handsome artist. When he came to visit, Naosuke cheerfully busied himself and helped the maids prepare special meals for him.
When she and the artist went out together, he saw them off
at the gate, smiling and looking happy.

"Let's go up the hill," the artist said during one of their
walks, "the view from the back garden of the foreigner's
mansion is really splendid. You can see all the mountain
ranges of Sagami and even Mount Fuji."

Sometimes they would ask Naosuke to come with them,
but he never did. "No thank you, I would rather go to look
for good fish for your dinner." There was, in his refusal, a
stubbornness that seemed to insist his domain was the river
and he had no business going anywhere else.

The river, seen from atop the cliff in the garden of the
foreigner's mansion, was lively and gay during the day-
time. Makeshift teahouses were constructed with bamboo
poles and bamboo lattice screens on the pebbles of the
riverbank. Red lanterns hung from their low roofs. A narrow, swift boat, with the same kind of red lantern on the
bow, went up and down the stream sounding drums to attract sweetfish. They could see Naosuke in his blue kimono,
walking quickly among the willow trees and evening prim-
roses on the bank, going from one fisherman to another.
They could hear his voice, "Do you have some small, young

sweetfish? You know, the size you can deep fry, bones and all."

Occasionally, the sun came out of the clouds and changed the color of the road by the river. Then the white caps radiated in gold. It appeared that Naosuke could not find fish that satisfied him. He was going upstream now, picking up this ford or that, and finally disappeared from view into the lonely bushes. A single bird flew low around the shore where his figure had disappeared. The bird and Naosuke became one.

"I wonder if there can be a relationship between a man and a woman that could be compared with two unglazed pots that have just been taken out of the kiln, and placed side by side," the artist said to her.

"You are familiar with Basho's haiku, aren't you?

'Spring is passing
Bird cries, and tears
In the eyes of fish.'

"This haiku somehow always makes me realize that in our world there is unfathomably deep sadness and grief that is beyond our comprehension," she told him. Neither of them realized it, but they were strangely touched and influenced by Naosuke, and this made them say things which did not make much apparent sense, and yet, they were expressing what they truly felt. Slowly they went down the hill from the foreigner's mansion. Her steps were stronger and steadier now; she was gaining back some of her normal healthy self.

At eighteen, she finished high school and soon married the artist from the big city.

They met quite often before they married, and one day the artist said to her parents, "I have decided to take my life more seriously; I would like to do something with it. For that I feel I need an anchor to hold me down. The rare, quiet quality your daughter has is the thing I have been looking for. She will be my anchor, my binding."

For three generations now his family had lived in the big city where their refined gentility had spread so widely that it almost evaporated like a light-hearted perfume. She felt on her part that perhaps to live like a lovely porcelain doll in his house in the city would harmonize well with the melancholic mood of her life.

"But how can it be love? Do they love each other? I don't understand it. . . " her brother protested. The father kept silent. Again, the mother was wisest. "It seems to me she will not bloom and become alive, unless she is well tended, coaxed and cared for. But, if that tending hand should be too strong, it might injure the sprout of her life. I think this young artist knows just how to care for her." The father who was listening to his wife with his arms folded opened his eyes and said, "Well, I think you are right. Call Naosuke. I want him to supervise the construction of a temporary bridge for the bridal procession of our daughter."

Naosuke worked hard everyday with the construction workers. It was late autumn and there was hardly any water in the ford. Red leaves came floating down on the river and piled up on the edges of fords or became trapped in the bamboo mesh of the gabions, withered and rotten. The far mountains could be seen very clearly, with blue-green creases indented in them. The water sounded white as it passed through a bamboo net set up to catch the sweetfish.

For several days before the wedding, she was confined in her room because her curly hair had to be straightened for the traditional hairdo of the bride. She could not see anyone during that time; neither could she see the river. Only once she talked with Naosuke through a closed *shoji* screen.

"How is the river?" she asked him.

"The river has become awfully thin these days." Naosuke's voice was flat and emotionless. It was the voice of a servant, no doubt, who obediently answered his mistress' questions.

Then, another morning Naosuke came to her room and, opening the screen just enough for the width of the book, quietly put the book of Greek mythology she had lent him on the *tatami* floor.

Naosuke was drowned in the river and died. It was only two weeks after her wedding day. The people thought it was an unhappy accident, and she believed this also. Yes, she had believed until yesterday. . . yesterday, she was reading the book of Greek mythology, and she found quite unexpectedly a sheet of paper between the pages of the book. The paper had turned yellowish from the dust of time. Something was written on it. It was a poem-like passage in Naosuke's hand. A horrible realization suddenly struck her ...could it be possible that Naosuke threw himself into the river and drowned? Was his death intentional? Was it a suicide? Did he kill himself?

The passage read:

I am building a bridge
The bridge she will cross.
Once she has crossed it, she will never cross back.

After I said farewell to her on the bridge
I, too, will never cross it again.

I wish the river would rise, and wash away the bridge. . . .

But, I hear the river god whisper—wash away yourself,
Not the bridge—

Ah, then, is the river a tomb?

That night, she dreamed of the river: The entire area was covered with snow. It was flat except for a few low mounds. The snow had stopped falling, but the oppressive grey clouds above were still impregnated with heavy snow. Both the sky and the land were vast and grey, but there were some uneven variations of the grey color in the sky as well as on the snow. In the middle of this vast land, a narrow river flowed. But when I came close to the river, I found it was not narrow at all, but wide and grand. It was the proportion of the river and the vast space that diminished the scale of the river. I was dressed like a hunter, a man. On the bank were a few reeds casting their thin shadows on the ground. I was walking with a rifle on my back, picking my steps among the reeds. Then the hunter was not I. It was Naosuke. I did not know, then, where I was or how I looked. I was not even sure if I existed or not; it did not matter to me. Only Naosuke, the hunter, bending his body forward, was striding. His steps were heavy. Then, I saw something else. It was a raft floating on the river, floating close to the shore where Naosuke was walking. They went at the same speed, in the same direction. I knew that raft came from the deep mountains of Chichibu where the river originated. The logs were either maple or willow, but all the bark had been peeled off, and they looked naked. The raft had two layers of logs. The upper layer was pale pink, it was the color of virginity; but the lower layer looked cold, it had a color of death....

Waking from the dream, she found herself talking to Naosuke, talking to him silently.

"Dear Naosuke, you have been dead for a long time. . . why did you come back to me? You were a hunter last night, you were walking along the river. But where? And for what purpose? What are you looking for? Are you still looking for something? Then, the river was not a tomb after all, was it? I know there are men and women in this world who can meet only by the river, with the river. . . ."

The river flows by her ear. The whitecaps of the waves remind her of the white teeth of a virgin from which no lie has ever come. She knows she will have to come even closer to the river, penetrate into the depth of its flow, of its mysterious consciousness.

1938